# THE COMPUTER AS A PAINTBRUSH

## Creative Uses for the Personal Computer in the Preschool Classroom

Janice J. Beaty

Elmira College

W. Hugh Tucker

Computer Consultant

MERRILL PUBLISHING COMPANY
*A Bell & Howell Company*
Columbus   Toronto   London   Melbourne

To the three- and four-year-old children of the Helm Nursery School who taught us and themselves how creative they could be with a computer.

Cover Photo: Bruce Johnson

Published by Merrill Publishing Company
A Bell & Howell Company
Columbus, Ohio 43216

This book was set in Serifa

Administrative Editor: Beverly Kolz
Production Coordinator: Linda Hillis Bayma
Cover Designer: Cathy Watterson
Text Designer: Cindy Brunk

Photo Credits: All photos copyrighted by individuals or companies listed. Merrill Publishing/photographs by Bruce Johnson, pp. viii, 54, 90, 110, and 162. All other photos by Janice Beaty.

Library of Congress Catalog Card Number: 86-61089
International Standard Book Number: 0-675-20523-9
Printed in the United States of America

1 2 3 4 5 6 7 8 9—91 90 89 88 87

# Preface

T his textbook presents a unique approach for using the computer as an activity center in the preschool classroom. The book describes how pairs of children can use the computer to enhance their social skills, cognitive skills, language development, and creativity through exploratory play. The text is designed for use by preschool teachers and college students in the fields of early childhood and education and child development.

While most textbooks about computers and young children tell teachers what they ought to do, this book tells them how. It gives readers guidelines on how to choose a computer based on the software they will need; how to sequence the use of the software according to its difficulty; and how to integrate computer programs into a comprehensive preschool curriculum. Ideas for using children's books, games, art, and materials are included for each piece of software discussed. In addition, the book provides the reader with a method for observing the developmental level of individual children as they use the various programs.

Because the text is based on original research in an off-campus early childhood setting, it includes numerous real-life examples of the ideas and concepts presented. Young children are described learning how to operate the various computer programs through exploratory play in which they extract the rules of the programs and then apply them. Readers are challenged to be as creative as the children in their own use of the computer in the preschool classroom.

No prior knowledge of computers is necessary for readers of this text. All technical terms are defined as they are used, and step-by-step directions for introducing the computer and each of the software programs are clearly stated. This book is especially appropriate for teachers and students who are not sure that the computer belongs in the early childhood classroom.

Novice computer users can explore the programs along with their children and should experience the same excitement when they discover that the computer really can be a paintbrush!

Because this use of computers with preschoolers is still in its beginning stages, the authors would appreciate hearing from readers who could share their own experiences with young children using computers. Please write to Janice J. Beaty, Elmira College, Elmira, New York 14901.

## ACKNOWLEDGMENTS

We wish to thank Bonny Helm, Director of the Helm Nursery School, and her teaching staff for allowing us to use their classrooms and children for our research. Thanks also go to Francine Halo, our research assistant; to Joe Fahs of the Elmira College Computer Center; to Ingrid Lindeqvist of the Gannett Trip Learning Center for her assistance in library research; to Phyllis Dyer, Marion Caplan, and Jeannie Berg and their children; to Beverly Kolz, Merrill Executive Editor, for her support and encouragement; to Computer Place at the Boston Museum of Science; and to the parents whose children are featured in the photographs. Finally, we would like to thank the reviewers of this text: Deborah Smith, University of Southern Mississippi; Mary A. Connolly, Sinclair Community College; Joyce Digby Gray, San Antonio College; Joan Isenberg, George Mason University; and Trisha Ainsa, University of Texas, El Paso.

*Janice Beaty and Hugh Tucker*

# Contents

# The Computer in the Classroom: Should You Let It In?

T he personal computer is no stranger to the preschool program. The latter years of the 1970s and the first half of the 1980s have seen an ever-increasing number of early childhood programs that have purchased computers and printers for use by their administrative and office personnel. There is no argument about the computer's benefits for helping programs to become cost-effective, keeping more accurate books and records, and writing grant proposals. The computer has more than earned its keep in the matter of time and money saved.

But does the personal computer belong in a preschool classroom? Should three- or four-year old children be exposed to such a highly technical tool? Won't it make robots of them, or at the very least, turn them into social isolates who do not know how to communicate with other children? Teachers who have "taken the plunge" and integrated the computer into their regular curriculum answer the question about robots and social isolates with a resounding "No!" Then they go on with an enthusiastic description of the learning and developmental benefits their children are deriving from their interaction with this unique learning tool. Terms like "social skills," "problem-solving skills," "new vocabulary," "creativity," and "equal opportunity for the disadvantaged," keep cropping up in their conversations. "Why," they exclaim, with the ultimate tribute, "the computer is even a paintbrush!"

Like many early childhood specialists who are "people persons," we had our doubts about computers in early education. Surely elementary school was early enough to introduce children to these marvelous mechanical monsters. But, no, we soon discovered "the earlier the better" was a rule as appropriate to learning the computer as it was to learning a second language.

Young children's brains, it seems, were naturally designed to absorb new ideas and relationships in the way that computer programs pre-

1

sent them. We already knew about children acquiring an entire language from scratch from birth through age five—without being formally taught. Then we began to understand that the computer presented its teachings in the same way: children could learn by playing around with ideas, by exploring and experimenting with them, by trial and error, by inducing the rules and then applying them, just as they did with their native tongue. Furthermore, learning in this exploratory way was said to be especially effective from birth through five years. This we had to see!

We began our quest by reading the literature, attending computer sessions at national conferences, and finally by implementing our own Elmira College Computer Project with two nursery school classes of 44 three- and four-year-old children for six weeks (see chapter 2). The results of our own computer project gave us an answer to the question: Should we let the computer in the classroom? Our response was a strong "How can we afford to keep it out?" The chapters of this book will describe our response in detail.

## SURVEY OF COMPUTERS IN THE PRESCHOOL

Various studies have looked at the uses of computers in the preschool. One that seems especially relevant to our interests surveyed a random sampling from a data bank of 58,000 licensed child-care centers around the country. Of the centers responding, 490 used computers. With respect to ownership, 75 percent said they owned computers, and 27 percent said they intended to buy one (or an additional one). Of the centers responding, 75 percent were preschools, 18.8 percent were day-care centers, 4.4 percent were Montessori schools, and 2 percent were Head Start centers.

The computers were used in various ways in the centers. Twenty-five percent of the centers used their computers for administrative purposes, 58 percent for recreational activities with children, and 72 percent for educational purposes. The centers used a variety of computers: 43 percent used Apple, 22 percent Commodore, 11 percent Texas Instruments, 10 percent Radio Shack, 8 percent IBM PC, and 6 percent other brands, including Atari and Franklin (Report on Education Research 1985, 6).

## ATTITUDES TOWARD COMPUTERS

### Children

How do the people feel who are already involved with computers in the preschool classroom? Children accept them wholeheartedly. At first they look at them as they would a television. Then they discover that these machines are not passive; they are interactive. In other words, children can make them do things, not merely watch them doing their own thing. It is a heady discovery.

## Parents

Parents have mixed attitudes depending on whether or not they own or use a computer. Mitchell (1984) found that of the forty-five parents responding to a questionnaire, 86 percent used computers at work. One-third of these families had computers at home as well, using them for word processing, financial programs, video games, and educational programs. Educational software such as alphabet programs, shapes, colors, creative graphics, paint programs, *Facemaker, Gertrude's Secrets,* and other reasoning programs for young children was owned by 71 percent of the families. According to 92 percent of the computer owners, the most important quality of the software was that the children could be in control. Young children in 64 percent of the families used the computer at least once a week and many used it daily.

Of the parents who owned computers, 64 percent had strongly positive feelings toward young children using the computer. None expressed fear or intimidation. By comparison, 30 percent of the nonowners expressed positive feelings about young children using the computer. Fear and intimidation was expressed by 15 percent of the nonowners. However, 70 percent of both groups wanted their children exposed to the computer. One interesting finding showed that nonowners ascribe more importance to the computer

*Children accept computers wholeheartedly when they discover that they can control them.*

than do owners. Of the parents who did not own computers 90 percent felt that their children would be at a disadvantage in society if they did not know about computers. By contrast, 70 percent of the owners felt that way. However, 100 percent of both groups felt that schools should provide the opportunity for children to learn to use the computer (Mitchell 1984).

## Teachers

Of all the people concerned with computers in the preschool classroom, teachers show the most anxiety and reluctance to become involved (Jorde, n.d.). Since it is teachers who are most responsible for the quality of the program, it is to teachers and student teachers that this book is primarily addressed.

A large number of the studies on computers in the preschool have been done by colleges and universities. Frequently these researchers use their own personnel rather than the classroom staff to teach the children how to operate the computer. Preschool programs associated with public schools often rely on the school computer specialist to assist them with the computer aspects of their own curriculum. Some programs, in fact, take their children to an outside computer center to use the machines. Other centers bring in trained parent volunteers to be computer aides. But many teachers without such resources to support their use of a computer simply have not considered bringing the computer into their classrooms at all.

It is now time for teachers and teacher-assistants to become directly involved with the use of a computer in their classroom. They need not worry that their supervision of computer activities will pull them away from their other classroom duties any more than the block area does, or the puzzle table. Young children quickly learn how to use the computer on their own. Nor do teachers need to worry about being unable to learn to use this seemingly complex machine. It is no more difficult than an electric typewriter. If three- and four-year-old children can learn to use the computer with ease, then their teachers will have no trouble. Furthermore, the classroom staff will be delighted to find out, just as children do, how much fun it is to operate the computer programs. The computer in the preschool classroom motivates all individuals to experiment in an entertaining and playful manner with visual ideas and concepts.

Women, it has been found, display lower levels of innovative behavior as well as more aversion to taking risks than do men. Furthermore, women have lower levels of confidence with respect to computer technology, which inhibits them from gaining the necessary experience with computers to break down their own negative attitudes (Jorde, 10). Because most early childhood teachers are women, such prejudices against computer technology show up strongly at the preschool level.

Math anxiety, which also disproportionately affects women and racial minorities, may have a bearing on why women show more hesitation than men about using computers (Jorde, n.d.). It is not math knowledge but typing skills that will help women to use computers effectively. Since more women than men possess typing skills, women should be able to perform computer tasks with great effectiveness—which, of course, they do when they become involved.

Women teachers owe it to the children in their classes to act as role models for using computers with ease and enjoyment. It is the attitude of preschool staff members toward the computer that sends important nonverbal messages to the children. If children see their teachers and aides using the computer with ease and enjoyment, they will want to do the same. On the other hand, if only the outside computer specialist uses the machine in the classroom, children may get the nonverbal message that their teachers either do not like computers or may be afraid of them.

## OVERCOMING COMPUTER ANXIETY

Reluctance in using the computer seems to be based on a fear-of-the-unknown type of anxiety. Persons who have had experience with similar kinds of equipment seem to be able to transfer their expertise to the computer without difficulty. For instance, secretaries who have used electric typewriters often can transfer their experience to computers with ease. Children also have no fear of the computer, partly because of previous experience: they think it is a television. Then they find out that the keyboard controls what happens on the "TV" screen and that they can control the keys. There is no fear in this discovery, only delight.

Teachers of young children can overcome their own anxiety and reluctance to use the computer in several ways. First, they can learn what others have done with the computer: how they choose the computer (hardware) and the programs (software) they use; how they set up the system; how they insert the programs and turn them on; what keys they press to run the programs; what they expect the children to do with the programs. To learn what others have done along these lines, teachers and student teachers can visit and observe preschool classrooms where the computer is being used. They can read books like this one that describe how to use the computer in the classroom. Finally, they will want hands-on experience with a computer themselves.

The best way to learn to use the computer is to try it out on your own. An experienced operator can get you started if you prefer, or you can learn on your own from a handbook or the directions that come with the machine or the program. You will want all of your classroom staff to become familiar with this electronic learning tool. Let each of them try all of the programs you have purchased, just as children do. After they are familiar with the basic operating procedures, let them explore each piece of software without reading the directions. Can they learn how each works by experimenting as the children do? Have them try to anticipate how the children will use each computer program before it is introduced. Then have them observe and record the children's responses to see if they guessed correctly. Learning to use the computer can be as enjoyable for the classroom staff as for the children.

## THE COMPUTER AND GENDER DIFFERENCES

Do boys use the computer more than girls? Are they better at it? Is there a difference between boys and girls using the computer in the classroom? Lipinski's 1984 study revealed concern over reports that school computer involvement was becoming a predominantly male activity. A number of researchers had reported greater male computer use in elementary and secondary schools. One stated that "among children ages 8, 9, 11, and 12, girls were never identified as computer experts" (Lipinski 1984, 5).

Such differences do not seem to show up at the preschool level we are happy to report. Studies of gender differences among preschoolers do not show young boys either dominating the computer or becoming more expert on it than girls. The opposite, in fact, is sometimes true. Lipinski (1984) found that the girls in her study spent significantly more time at the computer than did boys. In the Elmira College Computer Project we found that girls and boys showed equal interest and spent equal amounts of time on the computer, and that some of the most competent computer operators were girls.

We agree with Lipinski (1984) that computers should be introduced to children at the preschool level before such insidious sex stereotyping with respect to computers takes place. The potential for such stereotyping is all the more reason for the preschool staff, women and men, to learn to use the computer, thus serving as role models for their students. The computer plays too important a role in our society for it to become dominated and controlled by men. The time to prevent this from happening is at the preschool level before stereotyping takes place.

Furthermore, we are impressed with the nonsexist learning that can take place on the computer at the preschool level. For instance, girls, notoriously poor in math by high school level, can gain self-confidence in math skills through the use of preschool computer programs; while boys, who frequently encounter difficulty with verbal skills in the elementary grades, can gain competence in this area on the computer.

*At the preschool level, girls show as much interest in the computer as boys.*

## THE COMPUTER AS AN EQUALIZER

When we consider the amount of time, effort, and money spent by the government to ensure an equal opportunity and education for all children, we wonder whether anyone ever considered the personal computer "the great equalizer"? Think about it. Here is a powerful interactive learning device that presents a plethora of individualized programs to all children—white, black, rich, poor, Hispanic, Native American, handicapped, bilingual, slow learners, highly intelligent—to be used by each of them at his or her own speed to gain the skills, knowledge, and development necessary for a good life in the modern world. All we have to do is make sure all children are given equal access to these programs. Since low-income families may never be able to afford computers, it is up to the school to provide these high-tech tools for all children, no matter what their backgrounds.

For the slow learner the computer responds with unlimited patience. He or she can spend whatever time is necessary to acquire the skills taught by the computer program. On the other hand, the quick thinker will be challenged by accelerated versions or higher levels of the same program. Much computer software is programmed to respond to the individuals who use it. In other words, anyone can learn from it at his or her own level of development.

Lee (1983) notes that the learning style of black children favors visual, audio, and creative expressiveness, while schools value an analytical style "which is compatible with concentration alone for long periods of time, impersonal learning stimuli and other abstractions to be dealt with according to a schedule." Computer programs promise help for black children with learning difficulties by providing visual and auditory stimuli while enabling them to engage in analytical thinking.

Studies show that children from low-income families, handicapped children, and bilingual children also learn from computer programs what they had difficulty learning in regular classrooms. Again, it should be stressed that computer programs wait until their users understand the concepts the programs are presenting. Because computer programs can be chosen for the individual child, he or she can pursue them on an individual basis while the teacher responds to others in the class. With computer programs, disadvantaged children have access to a wide range of skills and information they might never encounter in a classroom without a computer. Because many affluent families already own home computers, the learning gap between the poor and the well-to-do child is bound to widen unless schools provide the difference. The difference of course can be the computer.

Another type of individual difference can be positively affected by the use of the computer in the preschool: that is the shy child who holds back and does not become involved in group activities. At times we assess such children as immature and not ready for group activities. At other times we find them to be loners, whose personality or psychological makeup will always keep them at the edge of the group. They may, of course, be quiet but highly intelligent children who are too unsure of themselves to attempt group activities. Computers in the preschool have been the saving grace for many of these children.

Two teachers have reported that social relations were reversed in their classrooms when computers were used. Formerly quiet, passive children became skilled on the computer, and one even emerged as a leader (Mitchell 1984). In our own Elmira College Computer Project we found the same thing to be true. Quiet, often immature-acting children blossomed on the computer.

## THE COMPUTER AND CREATIVITY

Because computer programs approximate the learning process that occurs naturally in children, they are especially effective during the early childhood years. Young children learn by interacting with objects and people in their environment. Computers are programmed to interact with their operators. Young children also learn best by the discovery method, that is, by manipulating things, trying them out, and seeing what they can do with them. Good computer programs are self-teaching devices that respond best to exploratory acts. Finally, young children are still in the visual thinking stage of their development. Computer programs for young children match this development by presenting concepts nonverbally in colorful graphics.

This visual type of thinking, which is especially prevalent during the early childhood years, seems to be tied to creativity. Anyone who has observed young children closely realizes how original they are in their thinking, speaking, and acting. It is almost as if they are inventing thoughts, words, and actions for the first time. The fact is that for themselves, they are. As psychologists like Jean Piaget have discovered, children use their experiences in the world around them to create their own knowledge (table 1).

The words children speak certainly resemble the words spoken around them, but young children use those words differently. Subconsciously they seem to extract the rules of the language, but then they apply them in their own original ways. Listen to children invent words when confronted with new situations. When a satellite came on the computer screen during the Elmira Project, one of the three year olds called it a "space ball."

Watch what young children draw at the easel or at the painting table. Experienced teachers realize that the children are not making a representational drawing in the beginning. They are only manipulating the medium of paint and experimenting with its effects. Nevertheless, some of their art products can be compared with the works of adult abstract expressionists. How can this be, we ask ourselves? What is it that gives young children such a fresh and original point of view? By the time most children are seven or eight years old this creativity seems to have faded away.

Specialists concerned with keeping creativity alive in adults or redeveloping creativity in those who have lost it have recently come up with new insights on the subject. Some of those insights definitely tie in with young children and the computer. Creativity does seem to be involved with visual thinking, that is, being able to create images in the mind's eye. Young children are able to think with images instead of words more easily than most older children and adults, probably because their verbal skills are not so highly developed. By the time they are seven or eight years old, much of their creativity has faded away because they have switched over to verbal thinking. After all, most children have by that time fully acquired their native language and have learned to read.

The functions of the two hemispheres of the brain become better defined as well during the early childhood period of development. Verbal skills are ultimately controlled by the left hemisphere in most people, while visual

**TABLE 1.** Piaget's stages of cognitive development

*Sensorimotor Stage*

*(Birth to age 2)*

Child thinks in visual patterns ("schemata").

Child uses senses to explore objects (i.e., looks, listens, smells, tastes, and manipulates).

Child learns to recall physical features of an object.

Child associates objects with actions and events but does not use objects to symbolize actions and events (e.g., rolls a ball but does not use ball as a pretend car).

Child develops "object permanence" (i.e., comes to realize an object is still there even when out of sight).

*Preoperational Stage*

*(Age 2 to 7)*

Child acquires symbolic thought (i.e., uses mental images and words to represent actions and events not present).

Child uses objects to symbolize actions and events (e.g., pretends a block is a car).

Child learns to anticipate effect of one action on another (e.g., realizes pouring milk from pitcher to glass will make level of milk decrease in pitcher as it rises in glass).

Child is deceived by appearances (e.g., believes a tall, thin container holding a cup of water contains more than a short, wide container holding a cup of water).

Child is concerned with final products (i.e., focuses on the way things look at a particular moment, "figurative knowledge," and not on changes of things or how things got that way, "operational knowledge"), and he cannot seem to reverse his thinking.

*Concrete-Operational Stage*

*(Age 7 to 11)*

Child's thoughts can deal with changes of things and how they got that way.

Child is able to reverse his thinking (i.e., has ability to see in his mind how things looked before and after a change took place).

Child has gone beyond how things look at a particular moment and begins to understand how things relate to one another (e.g., knows that the number two can be larger than one, yet, at the same time, smaller than three).

*Formal-Operational Stage*

*(Age 11 + )*

Child begins to think about thinking.

Child thinks in abstract terms without needing concrete objects.

Child can hypothesize about things.

Source: Janice J. Beaty, *Observing the Development of the Young Child.* (Columbus, Ohio: Merrill Publishing Co., 1986), 172. Reprinted with permission.
NOTE: Information from Forman, pp. 69–93 included.

imagery is controlled by the right hemisphere. Verbal and abstract thought thus become left hemisphere functions. Visual thinking may not be as useful to young people during the school years and thus loses its impact; with it goes creativity for many people.

Scott Kim, author of the highly original book *Inversions,* MIT Press, 1985, which is filled with words that say the same thing when they are inverted, declares: "Words are dominant over pictures in academic and serious circles because they're easier to produce, but computers like the Macintosh are changing that. To me, computers are the answer to getting visual thinking recognized" (Stewart 1985, 54). He and other creative designers believe that young children have active visual imaginations that they may be able to preserve instead of losing as they develop verbal skills. The computer may be the answer.

Yet if visually oriented computer programs are to be used for developing and preserving this precious creativity in people, they must be introduced early in the educational process while children are still in the visual thinking mode. This means that computer use should start in the preschool with programs selected for their strong visual appeal. Then such programs must be continued into the elementary and secondary school years.

There is an exciting future in store for our children. We cannot even imagine the new careers they may finally pursue when their formal education is completed. But we can help our children get a strong start by providing them with learning tools, such as the computer, to support the wide range of development that is every child's birthright.

## THE COMPUTER AS A LEARNING TOOL

Child development specialists have long understood that young children have within them the power to teach themselves. If we watch young children at play, we note that they frequently pretend about real things in order to see how things work or to learn what it is they have to do. Maria Montessori recognized this trait in children at the beginning of the century and designed all of the original learning materials for her classes as self-teaching devices that the young child could discover how to use on his or her own. Many of the early childhood educators who followed then set up activity areas or learning stations in their classrooms full of similar materials that children could learn from on their own. But the problem has always been one of matching the right materials with the right child.

Which materials are suitable for which children? A developmental toy, for instance, should be challenging but not too difficult for a child. Some puzzles are too simple, some too complex. Children in a classroom may engage in certain activities with pleasure at first, but later they may outgrow them. As we know, children often grow and develop at individual rates completely unrelated to their chronological age. How is the preschool teacher to keep up with the number of individual differences in learning levels present in every classroom? Most teachers respond by stocking their programs with games, toys, and activities at many levels of difficulty and leave it up to the child to choose the ones most suitable.

A single personal computer with a complement of appropriate programs can help to resolve the problem of matching challenging learning games with the individual child's level of learning. The chapters to follow will discuss the levels and difficulties of particular programs and suggest a sequence for introducing them to the children. Once the children are familiar with the programs available, they can select their own during the free play period. Many computer programs contain several games at increasing levels of difficulty to challenge the children who have mastered the beginning level games. Or, as Banet (1978) puts it: "Rather than prescribe a child's learning experience, the computer can present an inviting menu from which the child can choose, freeing him or her from adults' limited ability to prescribe optimal educational experiences."

An adult's limited ability to prescribe appropriate activities for individual children includes the difficulty teachers have in determining the child's readiness for certain activities. Is Jeffrey ready to encounter numbers as abstract symbols, for instance? Teachers frequently underestimate a child's ability to learn. Computers never do. The appropriate programs are there for the children to learn at their own level and at their own speed.

Does this mean that the personal computer will eventually replace the teacher in the preschool classroom? Not at all. Not any more than the block corner or the science area replaces the teacher. Teachers instead will be free to spend more time with individuals having special needs or with groups working with other activities. The computer is just one more of the many learning centers every classroom should contain.

Young children's original learning of concepts and skills, however, does not come from computer programs but from real experiences and active physical manipulation of things. Computer programs can be used in the preschool classroom to consolidate the learning children have acquired from concrete activities. *Jeepers Creatures,* a program using mixed-up animals, is an excellent follow-up for a visit to the zoo. *Stickybear ABCs* reinforces the ideas children have learned from the wooden alphabet-matching game they have been playing. "DRAW" from *Early Games for Young Children* gives preschool boys and girls a chance to practice the eye-hand coordination they have been trying out with crayons or felt-tipped pens.

If teachers select computer software wisely, they can integrate it into the total curriculum of the program to support and extend children's learning and development in ways that few other toys or activities can do. Because computer programs are interactive and give immediate feedback to their users, they can respond to individual children's learning needs, challenging them to extend their accomplishments and attempt higher level skills. The chapters to follow describe selected programs as examples of how children can pursue such individualized learning and how teachers can fully integrate these experiences into the curriculum.

## THE COMPUTER AND THE CHILD'S SELF-CONCEPT

Self-esteem for the young child in the preschool is promoted by people and activities that encourage success, independence, and good feelings about him- or herself. The personal computer can be a powerful tool in shaping such positive attitudes. First of all, children can learn on their own to be successful with computer software if the programs have been chosen with care. Through playful exploration of a program, children learn how it works and what it takes to use it successfully.

Good programs reinforce the correct responses from children. When children make mistakes, such programs ignore errors and do not respond. Thus, the young computer operators learn how to work the program as it should be done. In addition to gaining competence, they gain confidence in their ability to handle not only this adult-type tool, but also other learning activities. Success breeds success. Shy children who may have held back in other classroom activities are often the ones who gain such competence and, therefore, confidence from the computer.

In the words of Wright and Schwartz (1984), "That the child views him or herself as a person in control of the computer, underlies all of the experiences." Child development specialists understand that striving for control and independence plays a large part in the growth of preschool children who often feel helpless in the complex adult world around them. To be included in and feel control over an adult-type activity such as the computer can give the young child a feeling of self-confidence and self-worth that is seldom equalled through other experiences. Children who have been successful with computer programs often go on to more complex tasks than even their teachers felt were possible.

So—should you let the computer into your classroom? Only you can decide. The chapters that follow describe the ways computers can be integrated into the preschool classroom and the gains both teachers and young children can expect from their use.

## REFERENCES

Banet, Barnard. "Computers and Early Learning." *Creative Computing,* (September-October 1978): 90-94.

Beaty, Janice J. *Observing the Development of the Young Child.* Columbus, Ohio: Merrill Publishing Co., 1986.

Campbell, Patricia F., and Shirley S. Schwartz. "Microcomputers in the Preschool: Children, Parents, and Teachers." In *Young Children and Microcomputers,* edited by Patricia Campbell and Greta Fein. Englewood Cliffs, N.J.: Prentice-Hall, 1986.

Cuffaro, Harriet K. "Microcomputers in Education: Why Is Earlier Better?" *Teachers College Record* 85, no. 4 (Summer 1984): 559-68.

Forman, George E., and David S. Kushner. *The Child's Construction of Knowledge: Piaget for Teaching Children.* Washington, D.C.: National Association for the Education of Young Children, 1983.

Isenberg, Joan, and Marianne Latall. "Microcomputers in a Developmentally Based Program: Assets or Liabilities." Paper presented at the National Association for the Education of Young Children Conference, Los Angeles, November 1984.

Jorde, Paula. "Change and Innovation in Early Childhood Education: Research Survey." Evanston, Ill.: National College of Education, n.d.

Lee, Marjorie W. *Early Childhood Education and Microcomputers.* ERIC Document, ED 231 503, 1983.

Lipinski, Judith M., Robert E. Nida, Daniel D. Shade, and J. Allen Watson. *Competence, Gender and Preschooler's Free Play Choices When a Microcomputer Is Present in the Classroom.* ERIC Document, ED 243 609, 1984.

Mitchell, Edna, and Pat Monighan. "Computers in the Lives of Young Children and Their Families: Research Results and a Future Agenda." Paper presented at the National Association for the Education of Young Children Conference, Los Angeles, November 1984.

Nieboer, Ruth Ann. *A Study of the Effect of Computers on the Preschool Environment.* ERIC Document, ED 234 898, 1983.

*Report on Education Research.* "Preschoolers Getting Head Start on Computer Learning, Survey Shows," August 1985, 6.

Smithy-Willis, Deborrah, Mary Tom Riley, and Dale Smith. "Visual Discrimination and Preschoolers." *Educational Computer Magazine,* November-December 1982): 19.

Spencer, Mima, and Linda Baskin. *Microcomputers in Early Childhood Education.* ERIC Document, ED 227 967, 1983.

Stewart, Doug. "Teachers Aim at Turning Loose the Mind's Eye." *Smithsonian,* (August 1985): 44–55.

Taylor, Helen L. Sally. *Microcomputers in the Early Childhood Classroom.* ERIC Document, ED 234 845, 1983.

Wright, June, and Shirley Schwartz. "Researching the Microcomputer as an Integral Part of the Preschool Curriculum." Paper presented at the National Association for the Education of Young Children Conference, Los Angeles, 1984.

# Chapter 2

# The Computer in the Curriculum: Where Does It Belong?

T he computer is a powerful and flexible learning tool for preschool children. It can be used to teach number concepts, play music, tell stories—even as a paintbrush. Yet the flexibility, power, and expense of the personal computer has created a certain mystique around it that can distort its role in the preschool classroom. Some educators try to enshrine the computer; for example, computers may be placed in a separate computer room, or children may be taken to a computer center. This is expensive and unnecessary. The best use of the computer is to include it in the total curriculum.

Most teachers divide space into learning stations for dramatic play, blocks, books, large motor activities, manipulatives, water or sand play, wood-working, cooking, math, and science. The computer can be in a similar activity area of its own. During free play, children can explore favorite computer programs just as they can go to the block area or book corner. This book will show how a personal computer can be integrated into the total curriculum of the preschool and used creatively to further child development.

## THE COMPUTER

Computers come in many shapes and sizes, but all of them include three principal parts: the computer, the monitor, and the device for loading the program. These three parts are often separate but can be all one piece, as with the Apple Macintosh. A personal computer has a keyboard similar to a typewriter's. If the machine uses floppy disks for its programs, it may have one or two built-in disk drives, or the disk drive may be a separate piece of equipment. The display screen that shows the program looks much like a television set. A television set can, in fact, be used instead of a computer monitor to display computer programs.

One of the primary concerns adults have about children's use of computers is safety. Is it safe for children to use the computer and is it safe for the computer to be used by children? If a few simple rules are followed by both children and adults, using the computer is indeed a safe activity.

## Location in the Classroom

The first concern is the computer's location in the classroom. It should be placed against a wall near an outlet. A grounded (three prong) outlet will be needed for most computers. It is desirable to have the outlet and wires covered by a panel attached to the rear of the computer table. If this is not possible, the wires can be shielded by creative arrangements of toy shelves and other heavy, fixed furniture.

The computer station should not be placed in direct sunlight. Floppy disks (being made of magnetic tape) and computer chips can be damaged by extremes in temperature. Magnets or any magnetic toys used in the classroom should be kept away from the computer area and any software you may have purchased, because magnetic fields destroy data on tapes and disks.

The computer should be placed on a child-sized table or desk with two chairs in front of it, because two children will be using it at a time. Allowing the children to sit rather than stand while using the computer seems to provide them greater control and lengthen their attention span. Chairs convey the message that this is a serious activity.

One of the concerns of adults is the issue of object aggression (hitting the machine) (Shade 1983). Having the children sit seems to minimize this behavior. Placement of the chairs is very important. Both chairs should be placed evenly in front of the keyboard so that one child does not have a dominant position. It is easier to share control if one child is not placed off to the side of the computer.

The computer(s) should be placed in a sectioned-off, low traffic area. Access can be restricted with room dividers to minimize accidental damage from vigorous play. Many computer activities require concentration. Children are quite capable of concentrating; nevertheless, they are easily distracted by noise. Thus the computer area needs to be in a quiet part of the classroom.

## Television Sets as Computer Monitors

What about using an old television set as a computer monitor? There are a number of problems involved. First, the TV set may not work with a computer. The tuners in older sets may be worn out and, therefore, will not pick up the video signal from the computer. Second, although research on radiation from television sets is not conclusive, it is not wise to have children sit as close to old sets as they must with a computer.

*The computer should be placed on a child-sized table or desk with two chairs in front of it.*

Further, eyestrain is more likely to occur with larger TV screens than with a thirteen-inch color monitor or TV screen. The dots that make up the pictures on nineteen-inch screens, for instance, are larger and farther apart than on smaller screens. This distance makes focusing more difficult.

## INTRODUCING THE COMPUTER TO THE CHILDREN

The initial introduction between child and computer is crucial to the continuing relationship. Children need to be in control from the very beginning. If children are not allowed to touch the computer during the first session, they may be reluctant to use it during future sessions. With a few minutes of training, children as young as three can turn on the monitor and the computer. Monitors that have a button are easier to turn on than monitors with a knob. If you are using a disk drive with a separate switch, the child should also turn on that switch. Teachers who worry about young children being allowed to turn on such expensive equipment need to remember that children turn on the TV all the time.

In the first session, divide the class into groups of four to five children. Choose a program that uses most of the keyboard. It is important that something interesting happens when the child presses a key. *Kiri's Hodge Podge, Jeepers Creatures,* or an *ABC* program would all be good choices for this first session (see chapter 3).

If you are using a disk drive, have each child take a turn putting the disk into the drive and closing the disk drive door. You can relate the disk drive to a familiar experience by calling it a "garage" where the disk is kept. Show each of them how to hold the label on the disk between their thumb and fingers when they handle the disk. With the label up and their thumb on top they can place the disk into the disk garage and close the "garage door" without difficulty. If you are using a computer such as the Apple II, which loads the program from the disk when the computer is turned on, have each child turn on the monitor and the computer and watch the program appear on the monitor screen.

If you are using a computer such as the Commodore 64, which requires a loading command, have them turn on all units before putting the disk into the drive. At that time have each child practice typing in the command for loading the program. In the case of the Commodore 64, this is normally: LOAD "*,8,1". A better way to introduce the children to computers is to use a game cartridge program rather than the disk drive; Commodore and Atari, which have game cartridge ports, are good examples. You should have each child plug the cartridge into the game port and then turn on the computer. The important element is that the children should do everything necessary to operate the computer from the very beginning.

After the program has been transferred from the disk or cartridge into the memory of the computer, its graphics (pictures) will appear on the monitor screen. Children can then operate the computer by using the keyboard. Show them that they should use their "computer finger" (index finger) and only press one key at a time. Then have each one of them use the computer for a short period of time under adult supervision until they see how it works. As soon as they are comfortable with using the computer, step back and let them work the program on their own.

Control of the hardware (the computer) and software (the program disk, cartridge, or tape) by the child builds self-esteem. Children know computers are expensive. They know operating a computer is an adult activity. Doing it themselves develops confidence and a feeling of importance. If the children are not able to control most of the functions of both hardware and software with a minimum of adult supervision, then either the computer selected doesn't meet your needs or your supervision is too restrictive.

## RULES FOR USING THE COMPUTER

The principal guideline for creating rules is: Do not make too many of them! Surprisingly, children who have computers at home are more reluctant to use one at school than children who do not have computers at home. The reason is that parents who own computers are reluctant to let their young children use them without strict supervision. A rule that these children learn only too well is: Don't touch!

There are only a few rules that are necessary for the safety of the computer. The first rule is: No liquids in the computer area. This rule can be illustrated on a poster showing a glass of water with an X through it. Liquids spilled down an unprotected keyboard or into the ventilation slots of computer equipment can short out the equipment, causing a substantial repair bill.

The second rule is: Use only your computer finger. The computer finger is the child's index finger. The purpose of this rule is to prevent children from banging on the keyboard or pushing a number of keys at once. Because only one key can be pushed at a time, the child starts to discern what effect each key has in a particular computer program. This rule can be illustrated on a poster showing one finger on a key.

The third rule is: Come to the computer corner with clean hands. The reason for this is quite simple. Children need to touch all of the equipment, including floppy disks if you are using them. Sticky hands will soon make keys and disks unworkable. Keys are hard to clean, and disks can be damaged by trying to clean them. This rule can be illustrated by a poster showing hands under a faucet.

Rules should accentuate the positive. Negative rules discourage the child from using the computer. Furthermore, rules can be taught as you go along. For instance, let children choose who's next to use the computer by making a tag for each chair. When a child leaves the chair, he or she picks the next child by passing along the tag. Such self-regulation facilitates turn taking with a minimum of fuss and puts the children in control.

## THE COMPUTER IN THE CURRICULUM

Does the computer displace other important preschool activities, such as dramatic play or art? Although computers are a very attractive activity to many children, studies on the impact of computers on the curriculum indicate that participation in other classroom activities returns to previous levels after the computer has been in the classroom one to two weeks.

To illustrate, introduction of the computer into one preschool population caused a significant decrease in participation of art, blocks, and drama during the first week. However, by the second week art and blocks returned to the previous level of participation, although drama did not (Lipinski 1984, 3). Nieboer (1983, 22) found that after the initial disruption from the introduction of the computer, it became part of a balanced pattern of participation, with blocks and dramatic play remaining the most popular activities.

Controlling the number of children in the computer area provides an effective mechanism for encouraging pursuit of other activities. The Elmira Project found no displacement of other activities when two children self-regulated their time on the computer and others looked on whenever they chose.

While some studies (Shade 1983) indicate that the best ratio is one computer to ten children, most preschools have only one computer. Children like to work at the computer in small groups. Two children at the keyboard with other children watching and making suggestions seems the optimum. Free-play periods can be used for exploring favorite programs, while small-group activity periods can be used for introducing new programs. In either case, the computer is integrated into the total program of the preschool.

The computer does not replace any of the traditional activities of the preschool. But it does offer another avenue for pursuing what we have come to call "the three M's" of early child development: manipulation, mastery, and meaning.

## Manipulation

The computer fosters eye-hand coordination and fine motor skills. The children learn how to find and push the proper keys to achieve a goal. They may learn how to manipulate a joystick, to draw a picture, or to move objects around a screen—a fairly complex level of eye-hand coordination. They may draw lines through a series of key presses. The various ways to explore with the computer build new motor skills for the preschool child.

## Mastery

Children move quickly from exploration of the program to a level of mastery. At the mastery level children begin to understand cause and effect relationships. They know pressing a certain key provides a predictable result. They begin to search systematically for features of the program. The mastery stage is important for helping build self-esteem and autonomy. During this stage, children replace adult teachers as the primary source of expertise. Children at the mastery level begin teaching other children who are at the previous level, manipulation.

### Meaning

The final and most exciting stage in learning to use software is meaning. At this stage children "own" the software. They begin making up stories about what they see on the screen. They invent games when they discover how to control a specific graphic. The meaning stage is almost always developed as a group activity. It represents what Piaget refers to as "symbolic representation." When various authors refer to the computer as an avenue for symbolic representation, it is this third stage of development that is being discussed (Ziajka 1985, 61–66; Nieboer 1983).

## ADULT INTERVENTION

As with most skills, adult guidance will be needed to introduce a new program. Instruction on how to use the program helps the children move quickly from manipulation to mastery. However, it is important to withdraw direct supervision when the program has been mastered. When an adult is watching, children continuously look to the adult for confirmation that they are proceeding properly. Being present in the area while not directly supervising the activity indicates to the children that *you* know that they can operate the computer properly. Once this level of trust has been reached, the children become proud of their achievement. They see the computer as "hard" (difficult), and because they have succeeded at something "hard," they have pride in their work (Nieboer 1983).

## THE ELMIRA COLLEGE COMPUTER PROJECT

The Elmira College Computer Project provided many of the findings for this book. The project was located in a private preschool in Corning, New York. The preschool's long, window-lined classroom was divided into activity areas, and there was a separate gymnasium for large-motor activities. Twenty-four four-year-old children attended from nine until twelve o'clock on Monday, Wednesday, and Friday mornings. On Tuesday and Thursday, 20 three-year-old children attended during the same hours. Because the project was held the last six weeks of the school year, a number of the children had reached their next birthday.

     Activity areas included a book corner, a block corner, a dramatic play area with dress-up clothes and kitchen equipment, an area for learning toys and games (toy cash registers, wooden letters and numbers, puzzles), two painting easels, and an area with child-sized tables for art work and snacks. Low storage shelves separated each area. Colorful rugs covered several sections of the floor.

     About six weeks before the computer project began, an area for a play office with a working typewriter and a toy telephone was added. The purpose of the typewriter was to provide the children with experience in using a machine with a keyboard similar to the computer's.

The primary objective of the project was to observe how preschool children actually use a computer. A second objective was to test ways to integrate the computer into the preschool program. The basic methodology for the second objective consisted of finding or designing off-computer activities which would complement and supplement the software chosen for the project. A complete description of this process can be found in the following chapters.

The methodology chosen was that of using a participant-observer. An early childhood major in her senior year of college was placed in the classroom as a member of the teaching staff for the six-week period. During the free play and activity periods, she was responsible for the computer area; during the circle time, she introduced new computer programs, read stories related to the computer activity of the week, or introduced new games related to the computer program.

During computer activity periods, she provided initial instruction on how to use the program and then withdrew to become an observer as soon as the children were comfortable with the program. A checklist was provided for observing skill levels, interaction between the children, and use of software. In addition, a tape recorder was placed beside the computer to record the children's conversations. We visited the classroom two to three days a week to observe the project. We also met with the participant-observer twice a week to discuss findings and curricular strategies and to evaluate the progress of the project.

The computer chosen for the project was an Apple II + with a color monitor and disk drive. The Apple II + was chosen because of the large amount of good early childhood software available for the Apple II series. Apple II + computers were also available for long-term usage because the college had replaced Apple II + 's with Apple IIe's for undergraduate instruction, thus releasing Apple II + 's for other academic projects. The software used in the project will be described at length in other chapters.

## GUIDELINES FOR SELECTING A COMPUTER SYSTEM

### Buying a Computer

Buying a computer system (hardware) for a preschool program is a big decision. Most preschools operate on a limited budget, and even a low-priced computer is a major budgetary item. Nevertheless, the value of this interactive tool for individual or group learning and development is so great that preschool teachers and administrators need to weigh carefully whether monetary considerations alone will dictate curriculum practices and child development policies.

The first step in buying a computer is to identify creative software which can be integrated into a balanced preschool curriculum (see chapter 10). The software for the computer contains the programs the children will be using. Computer software comes in the form of cartridges, tapes, or floppy disks. These programs are in some ways similar to a record or tape for a record player. Unfortunately, not every program fits every computer. Too many people purchase computers first without regard to the software they will want to use. Then they are often restricted to a limited number of software programs that will fit only their particular computer. Thus, it is important for preschool programs to decide upon the software first because of the limited selection of quality computer software programs for preliterate children, and also because the expense of a library of software can eventually equal the cost of the computer.

Each of the chapters to follow will discuss specific examples of creative software for particular curriculum areas, as well as list at the end other available software programs.

Fortunately, most preschool software programs are available for computers in the lower price brackets. Preschool programs are available for the Apple II series, the Atari, the Commodore 64 and 128, and IBM-compatible personal computers. Many major software manufacturers, in fact, have similar versions of the same program for all four of the above-named computers. On the other hand, software produced by small companies may be available for one brand of computer only. Thus, you must find out at the outset which computers can accommodate the software you would like to use with children. If the software you have chosen will operate on only one brand of computer, then that is the brand of computer you must buy. On the other hand, if the software you have chosen is available for a number of brands of computers, then you will have a wider range of computers to consider. Your choice in the second case must be made on considerations other than that of software alone.

If possible, find a computer store or, better yet, a preschool where you can try out with children the software you are considering. If you can find a store that will demonstrate and support its products, it is worthwhile to pay a little extra for after-sale support, such as instruction in using programs, replacing damaged disks, and previewing new programs.

## Example Software Buyer's Table

To decide which computer to buy on the basis of software alone, you may want to preview various computer programs first and then make a list of possible software along with the types of computers on which they will operate (table 2).

**TABLE 2.**   Example software used in the Elmira college computer project

| Example Software | Type | Computer Compatibility |
| --- | --- | --- |
| Jeepers Creatures | disk | Apple, Atari |
| Hodge Podge | disk | Apple, Atari, TRS-80, I, II |
| Stickybear series | disk | Apple, Atari, Commodore 64 |
| Dinosaurs | disk | Apple, IBM, Acorn, Commodore 64 |
| Early Games for Young Children | disk | Apple, Atari, IBM, Commodore 64, VIC-20, TRS-80, I, II |
| Learning with Leeper | disk | Apple, Commodore 64 |
| Facemaker | disk | Apple, Atari, IBM, Commodore 64 |
| Picture Programming | disk | Apple |

From this particular list the computer buyer would probably decide to buy an Apple computer with a disk drive and, of course, a color monitor, since all of these programs are in color. A second choice would be an Atari or a Commodore 64, but then several other programs might need to be substituted.

## Game Cartridge Computers

The minimum system you could choose is a computer with game cartridge capacity and a color monitor. Although most personal computers can accommodate monochromatic (black-and-white, green-and-black, or amber-and-black) monitors, virtually all programs written for young children require color. Most computers can be attached to a color TV set; however, a computer color monitor normally has a sharper picture and the additional advantage of not having a station dial to adjust. If a color TV set is used, it should be small enough to be placed on top of or behind the computer (depending upon the brand). This minimum system can be obtained for less than $600.

The game cartridge solution limits you to programs that are available in game cartridge format only. It also limits the choice to computers such as the Atari and the Commodore which have built-in game ports. In addition, many programs are not available in game cartridge format. The majority of programs for young children, in fact, are available on floppy disks rather than game cartridges.

## Tape Recorder Computers

Another possibility is to buy a computer which uses a tape recorder for storing its programs. Many programs are available on tape for a number of computers. This storage medium, while cost-effective, is not recommended for preschool programs. Tapes are more fragile than either cartridges or floppy disks. The tape recorders used for storage are more difficult to use and less reliable than either cartridges or floppy disks. Tape programs take longer to load into a computer; making it frustrating to the young child, who has little patience when waiting to use the computer.

## Disk Drive Computers

Almost all preschool computer programs are available on floppy disks. A floppy disk is a round piece of magnetic tape, about the size of a 45-rpm record, enclosed in a square cardboard envelope. The advantage of a floppy disk over tape is that the computer can go directly to the game chosen rather than having to read through a series of games to find the proper one. A program that might take three minutes to load from tape can be loaded in a few seconds from a floppy disk. Young children can be taught to use floppy disks in a much shorter period of time than they can be taught to use tapes. An advantage of floppy disks over game cartridges is a greater choice of programs.

Floppy disks require a disk drive to read the program into the memory of the computer. Some computers such as the Apple IIc, the Apple Macintosh, the IBM PC, or the Commodore Amiga have a disk drive built into the computer; others require a separate accessory.

The initial cost of a computer should not be the sole criterion for choosing a computer for a preschool program. Other factors that should be considered are ease of use, expandability, and reliability.

## Ease of Use

Personal computers vary in ease of use. The Commodore 64, for instance, has a complex keyboard which could create confusion for the preschool child. Each key has four functions: uppercase, lowercase, and two sets of graphics. Because it has several keys that work differently from other computers, the Commodore keyboard will not prepare children for using other computers.

Another area of complexity with the Commodore 64 is the disk drive. Most computers use a disk-operating system that recognizes a "turnkey program," a program automatically loaded when the disk drive is turned on. The Commodore requires a keyboard command to load a program from the disk drive. Although young children can be taught the proper sequence of commands, it does provide an extra area for confusion. On the other hand, the Commodore provides an excellent set of graphic, color, and sound options for preschool programs. It is important for the buyer to look at these advantages and disadvantages before making a decision.

The Apple II computer is probably the easiest to use, and it is available with a broad base of software. An Apple II uses a standard computer keyboard and provides for turnkey operation of the disk drive system. If a preschool budget is tight, one solution would be to buy a secondhand Apple II +, with a disk drive. The Apple II +, although no longer manufactured, will run virtually all preschool software designed for Apple II computers.

The IBM PC is another option. However, the cost of the IBM PC is probably prohibitive for most preschool programs unless one is available secondhand or on loan. There are a large number of programs for preschool children, all of which will run on the IBM PC. Normally these programs will require a procedure for installing the BASIC language and other system files prior to use in the classroom. The procedure requires moving the programs from the PC DOS disk to the preschool program disk either by copying them with the COPY command or by using an Install program supplied on the preschool disk. If either is necessary, explicit directions will be provided in the documentation accompanying the program.

A new generation of computers reaching the market from Apple, Atari, and Commodore promises easy-to-use, powerful programs for the preschool child. The Apple Macintosh, the Atari 520ST, and the Commodore Amiga have powerful capabilities with easy-to-use programs for the preschool child.

One of the more exciting aspects of the new generation of computers is the speed and memory that make it possible to build easy-to-use drawing and music programs. The increased memory and power of the new generation of computers should encourage the development of programs that use spoken words for both commands and interactive stories for preliterate children. The Commodore Amiga includes speech generation software that can be used to translate written words into spoken words.

## Expandability

A second criterion for buying a computer is expandability. Will you be able to add external devices if they are needed for a program? If you decide to buy a printer, will you be able to buy from a variety of vendors or will you be limited to printers merchandised only by the computer manufacturer? Certain types of printers can be used to print out children's drawings and paintings if this seems important to you (see chapter 8).

Does the computer have a joystick port? Many preschool programs either require or allow the use of a joystick. A joystick is a small hand-held device usually attached to the computer by a long cord. By moving the stick, a person can control objects on the computer screen. Most commercial electronic games use a joystick for control. Joysticks can be used to move objects around on the screen, to paint pictures, or to make selections from a menu of choices on the screen.

Other selection devices are touch pads, light pens, the mouse, and touch screens. Chapters 8 and 10 provide a more extended discussion of the uses and limitations of such devices.

## Reliability

The final factor to consider when buying a computer is reliability. There are three aspects of reliability to keep in mind. The first is company reliability. Will the computer continue to be supported by the manufacturer? Some companies are very careful to maintain upward compatibility with new computer models. This means that software written for previous models will run on new models of the computer line. Examples of computers with upward compatibility are Apple and Commodore. Programs written for Apple II computers will run on the Apple IIc. However, not all programs written for the Apple IIc will run on older Apples. In the case of Commodore, VIC 20 programs will in some cases run on the Commodore 64, and Commodore 64 programs will run on the Commodore 128. However, programs designed specifically for the Commodore 128 will not run on the VIC 20 or the Commodore 64. Upward compatibility is important in preventing rapid obsolescence of the computer. Some companies produce a series of incompatible computers, creating programs for one model which will not run on other models in their computer line.

Another thing to watch for when determining a company's reliability is the discontinued manufacture of a particular series of computer being purchased. Such computers are referred to as "orphan computers" (e.g., Adam from Coleco). Such computers may be appropriate in situations where computer literacy or programming is being taught, but not in a preschool setting. The preschool uses of computers depend heavily on the continued production of high-quality software for the specific computer being used.

The second aspect of reliability is the repair record of the computer. Talk to educators at other institutions about the reliability of the computers they own. If you discover that a high percentage (20 percent or greater) of a particular brand of computer breaks down within a year of purchase, your preschool program should avoid that computer.

The third aspect of reliability is one of time. If the computer should break down, how long will it take to repair it? Some computers can be repaired at the local dealer where they were purchased. Other computers have to be sent to the manufacturer or a regional repair center. Repairs that can be done at a local store often can be made within one to two days. Computers that have to be sent away for repair can be gone for as long as two months. In a nine-month program, this can represent a significant loss in the curriculum.

At the time of purchase it is wise to negotiate arrangements for repair services. If a repair will take longer than two days, try to have an understanding that a substitute computer will be supplied during repair period. It is often worthwhile to pay full retail price for this level of service and after-sale support. Computers purchased at a discount store often do not include such services.

The computer buyer's checklist can be used by preschool programs to help select the machine which best fits the usability, expandability, and reliability criteria from a sometimes overwhelming array of new computers (table 3).

## Computer Dealers

If you do not have a resident computer expert, the selection of a good dealer can be as important as the selection of the computer itself. Although it is less expensive to order from mail-order houses, a good local dealer can offer after-sale support not available from a mail-order house. Try to choose a local dealer who will provide after-sale support for the hardware and will demonstrate software prior to its sale. No dealer can carry all of the software available for a given computer, but he or she can allow you to preview the software that is in stock before it leaves the store. The dealer also should be the primary provider of warranty service. Try to find a dealer who will replace or quickly repair software or hardware that fails to operate during the manufacturer's warranty period. Try to avoid dealers who require you to deal directly with the manufacturer for warranty service.

**TABLE 3.**   Computer buyer's checklist

*Usability*

_____ Capital letters and numbers are printed without shifting

_____ Disk drive automatically loads programs

_____ Wide range of software is available

*Expandability*

_____ Printers of several makes are available

_____ Joystick port is built-in

_____ Touch pads, touch screen, light pens, mouse can be used

*Reliability*

_____ Computer runs both old and new software produced by company

_____ Computer continues to be manufactured

_____ Computer can be repaired easily and quickly

Computer hardware and software are extremely reliable, but, as for any manufactured product, it is wise to make plans for those times when things go wrong. Most defects will show up during the first ninety days of use. Reasonable precautions can prevent many problems.

## CHAPTERS TO FOLLOW

Each of the chapters in this book will illustrate how computer programs work with other elements of the preschool program to help children learn about and shape their world. Each chapter will discuss how computer programs can enhance the use of games, books, and other preschool activities. As the child's competence in using the computer increases, creative applications will emerge. Often these creations of the child will move in unexpected directions. The computer is one more tool for helping children discover the rules of the world they live in. As Burg (1984, 28) puts it: "It will not replace other activities but it can provide children with developmentally appropriate experiences." Even more important, using a computer is an activity that most children enjoy. Preschool programs with computers consistently report that it is a favorite activity for children.

## REFERENCES

Burg, Karen. "The Microcomputer in the Kindergarten: A Magical, Useful, Expensive Toy." *Young Children* 39, no. 3 (March 1984): 28–33.

Dreyfus, Hubert L., and Stuart E. Dreyfus. "Putting Computers in Their Proper Place." *Teachers College Record* 85, no. 4 (Summer 1984): 578–601.

Lipinski, Judith M., Robert E. Nida, Daniel D. Shade, and J. Allen Watson. *Competence, Gender, and Preschooler's Free Play Choices When a Microcomputer Is Present in the Classroom. ERIC Document,* ED 243 609, 1984.

Nieboer, Ruth Ann. *A Study of the Effect of Computers on the Preschool Environment.* ERIC Document, ED 234 898, 1983.

Ross, Steven M., and Larry Campbell. "Computer-Based Education in the Montessori Classroom: A Compatible Mixture?" *T.H.E. Journal,* (April 1983): 105–109.

Shade, Daniel D., Gloria E. Daniel, Robert E. Nida, Judith M. Lipinski, and J. Allen Watson. *Microcomputers: A Close Look at What Happens When Preschool Children Interact with Age-Appropriate Software.* ERIC Document, ED 243 6608, 1983.

Spencer, Mima, and Linda Baskin. *Microcomputers in Early Childhood Education.* ERIC Document, ED 227 967, 1983.

"Tracking Down the 'Right' Computer," *Electronic Learning,* (January 1984): 39–49.

Wright, June L., and Shirley S. Schwartz. "Researching the Microcomputer as an Integral Part of the Preschool Curriculum." Paper presented at the National Association for the Education of Young Children Conference, Lost Angeles, 1984.

Ziajka, Alan. "Microcomputers in Early Childhood Education? A First Look." *Young Children* 38, no. 5 (July 1985): 61–67.

# The Computer
# as a Playmate

C hildren's play is not just for fun. It is the means by which young children learn. It is the method by which they teach themselves about the world around them. Through play they manipulate or explore anything and everything they encounter in order to learn what it is about—but not deliberately. The learning, like the play itself, is spontaneous.

Look at young children at play. See how intensely they pursue it, how seriously they treat it. Watch the little girl or boy building a garage out of blocks for the new car or taking the baby doll "to the doctor's for a shot." It is as though play is their life's real work. For children it is. Young children around the world use play as the means for figuring out their environment. Whenever they encounter something new, they playfully explore it. They try it out in a playful manner to see what it is, how it works, and what they can make it do.

Because play seems such an unimportant juvenile pastime, adults often fail to understand its implications in child development. Adults view play as recreation or entertainment. But, for children, play is the vehicle through which they make sense of their world—through which they learn by teaching themselves. Every child is "programmed" at birth to approach the world playfully. They continue to do so as long as adults allow and encourage such exploration.

Preschool teachers who understand the value of play try to incorporate it into every aspect of their curriculum. They realize children learn best through their own playful interaction with their environment, rather than the teacher's formal teaching of subject matter. Such teachers keep their eyes open for new toys, implements, equipment, or activities with which their children can interact and learn from. The personal computer is such a tool.

## THE COMPUTER AS A PLAYMATE

Children usually recognize the computer as a playmate long before adults do. They are accustomed to seeing such interesting equipment in their environment. They see television sets and typewriters and other fascinating adult implements around them. They would love to get their hands on such machines to play around with them, to try them out and see what they will do. They are not concerned with making mistakes or breaking them. Such constraints are not a part of playful exploration. Nor does the fact that they do not know how such machines work bother these young explorers. Just give them a chance and they will learn how by trial and error, by making a guess, or by just plain fooling around.

When a computer enters the preschool classroom, children eye it with the same interest. They can't wait to get their hands on it, unless they have been previously restrained. Adults, on the other hand, know too much about the world to feel the same thrill about exploring the unknown. They know, for example, how much such an instrument costs. They worry that it might be broken if used incorrectly. Because many adults do not know how to use the computer, they do not feel free to touch it without reading the directions or receiving instructions from someone else. Adults do not use play as their principal mode for learning. The thought that the computer is an instrument children can and should play around with fills them with astonishment or horror.

Yet, such is the case. Computers are remarkably sturdy machines. Sticky fingers or spilled liquids are the only potential hazards. Otherwise, both children and adults should be encouraged to explore and experiment freely with these remarkable machines.

Children will be delighted to learn that the computer, though it has a typewriter keyboard, does much more exciting things than just print letters. They also will be pleased to learn that the monitor, though it looks like a television set, does much more than show them pictures.

Teachers who welcome the computer into their classrooms will be amazed at how easily their children learn through play to interact with computer programs. They will be more delighted when they realize the powerful tool they have taken on as a partner to promote the development of their children's social skills, language skills, cognitive concepts, problem-solving skills, creativity, and self-concept. Such teachers should not worry whether they themselves understand the computer. Their children will soon be teaching them!

## GETTING STARTED

Some teachers set the stage for bringing a computer into the classroom by starting with a typewriter. A used manual typewriter works better than a child's play typewriter. The machine can be set up on a low table with paper nearby. At least two chairs should be used for the children because they will treat the typewriter as a group activity. If only one chair is used, children usually ignore it and stand in front of the machine, thus encouraging too many children to cluster around. On the other hand, if you require children to use the typewriter one at a time, you will miss an exceptional opportunity for spontaneous peer teaching and social interaction.

Remember, these are preliterate children who are only playing at typing in the beginning; they are not trying to type real words. After all, most of them do not know how to spell any words other than their names. In fact, they seem to get as much pleasure out of using the typewriter without paper as they do with paper.

Then what is the point? you may ask. What are children supposed to be learning, if not to type words? Children will be learning that pressing

*Some teachers set the stage for bringing a computer into the classroom by starting with a typewriter.*

only one key at a time makes a letter appear (cause and effect); that pressing several keys at once jams the keys (incorrect operation); that the shift key makes capital letters; that the space bar makes a sound when pressed but makes only spaces between letters; that turning the roller makes the line of letters go up or down; that the typewriter bell dings at the end of the line; that pushing the return lever or moving the carriage starts a new line. Children can learn all of these operations by themselves through playful exploration. Because they are participating in a group activity, they will also learn the social skill of taking turns. Once they have mastered the mechanics of the typewriter, they will begin playing roles, pretending, and making up their own games.

The purpose of having a typewriter in a preschool classroom is not to teach the children to become typists, but to give them an opportunity to explore and learn the properties of a new implement; to draw conclusions about what it can and cannot do; to hone their small motor skills. Later, they will learn to recognize letters and find them on the keyboard when they need them.

Because the computer has a typewriter keyboard, using a typewriter first is a fine introduction to the computer. The skills and knowledge children need to develop apply to both implements.

The computer should be introduced, then, just as the typewriter is. Place it on a low table near a wall outlet so that its cords can be plugged in easily and kept out of the children's reach. A list of rules on the wall nearby is advised (see chapter 2). Two child-sized chairs seem to control the number of children using the machine at once. There is really not room for more than two to sit at the keyboard.

A small-group approach seems best. Introduce the computer by gathering three or four children around the machine while two children sit in the chairs. Name and point to the parts of the machine the children need to know at first: the keyboard, the monitor, the disk drive. Learning other terms at this point is unnecessary. Show the children how to hold the program disk carefully at one end and let the child sitting closest insert the disk into the disk drive or, as children like to call it, the "garage."

The child sitting on the left can then turn on the monitor and computer. Depending on the program and computer, the children may be able to start right away, or they may need further instructions.

The adult in charge should give minimal instructions. Use simple programs at first and let the children figure out how they work. If they ask you what to do, ask them what they think they should do or suggest they press a key and see what happens. Hitting the keys too hard or abusing the equipment is, of course, not in order. They should have learned to refrain from such behavior while using the typewriter. If they have forgotten, remind them.

Children also need to learn to "open the garage door," remove the disk, place the disk into its envelope and then into the program container, and turn off the monitor and computer. It is best to use only one program until all of the children are familiar with the equipment.

Similar small groups can be instructed in the same manner until everyone in the class has been introduced. Don't wait until all have been introduced to let anyone use it. Children need to apply their new knowledge immediately. Let them use the computer as soon as it has been introduced. The sooner they use it, the more comfortable they seem to be with it. They

*The teacher introducing the computer should gather a few children at a time around the machine.*

will not be comfortably familiar with the computer until they have tried it several times. Have the computer available every day during free play.

## SOCIAL SKILLS

For adults the computer is a one-person tool. It seems obvious to us that one person should sit in front of the computer and operate it by him- or herself. Why should it be different for young children? We have to remember that preschool children are not learning to become computer operators.

As with the typewriter, the reasons we bring the computer into the classroom have little to do with training the children to become skilled operators. It is the same as with other classroom activities. We promote and encourage block building, not for children to learn to be carpenters, masons, or architects. We have cooking in the classrooms, not for children to learn how to cook. We introduce the typewriter, not for children to learn typing. Rather, these activities are learning tools to help children achieve physical, cognitive, language, social, emotional, and creative growth.

It is the same with the computer. This tool is especially powerful for promoting social skills—if the learning center is set up properly. Research has shown that whenever more than one child at a time is permitted to use the computer the social skills of turn taking, turn waiting, and helping one another occur. (Isenberg 1984; Wright 1984; Sweetnam 1982; Borgh and Dickson 1986; Jewson and Pea 1982; Watt 1982; Nieboer 1983; Sheingold 1981).

The Elmira College Computer Project, which used the computer in one class of 20 three year olds and one of 24 four year olds, had similar results. In all cases, children worked on the computer together, talked, manipulated their turn taking, and taught one another how to use the program or the machine. Only Barnes and Hill (1983) warned that the microcomputer would lead young children to become social isolates; however, we have seen no evidence of such consequences and cannot foresee any, unless the teacher sections off the computer area and allows only one child to use it at a time.

We suggest that teachers take advantage of the drawing power of this unique learning tool and allow two children to sit at the keyboard at one time. A few others can watch and comment. Let the two users work out their own turns and their own methods for using the various programs. They need to be able to explore their options freely and playfully in order to discover how the computer works.

A child should be able to work from ten to twenty minutes at a time on the computer if so desired. Then another child may take a turn. Some classrooms use self-regulating devices such as necklaces, name tags, or hooks and tags to determine who and how many can play in an activity center at one time. Because the computer is one of the more popular classroom activities, we have found that a self-regulating device makes it accessible to those who want to use it, yet keeps it under the children's control. Occasionally the teacher may have to ask two children to exchange turns with someone else when they have been at the computer overly long. Fairness generally prevails. When children understand they are in control, they do not object to giving turns to others who are waiting.

Even in elementary school, children using computer interact with their classmates around it. Mary-Alice White, director of the electronic-learning laboratory at Columbia University's Teachers College (cited in Sweetnam, 1982), finds that not only do students interact more around the computer, they also cooperate more than during regular classwork. Other observers note that children often leave the computer if nobody else is there. It's no fun alone, they seem to be saying (Sweetnam 1982).

Preschoolers feel the same way, the Elmira Project showed. When only one child was on the computer, he or she did not spend as much time there as when there was more than one. With the three year olds, conversation kept them at the computer longer than when there was no conversation.

Turn taking and its regulation by the children were fascinating to observe. Certain children seemed to dominate at first. We observed one girl who completely dominated her partner when seated at the keyboard during her first attempt with the computer. Rather than take turns, she became so engrossed in the program that she insisted on being the first to press the keys. When others used the computer, she stood nearby and tried to reach over and push the keys. She could not seem to get enough of the experience. Imagine our surprise on the second day, after she had played the computer game for awhile, when she looked around, noted how many children were waiting for a turn, and said: "Well, I've been playing long enough. Let me let somebody else take a turn."

The children waiting for turns during free play on the second morning told others who came by to see what was happening: "We can't play. You have to have a necklace on to play." They then waited patiently for someone to finish and hand them the necklace.

The children eventually worked out their own way to take turns. For *Jeepers Creatures* they discovered that it took three keys to make the animal figure, so they allowed each other to make three key presses at a time.

## ATTENTION SPAN

It is interesting to note the effect that computer play has on attention span. Although three- and four-year-old children usually do not have long attention spans, they seem transformed while using the computer. Individuals tend to remain on the computer for extended periods of time. Some children involved in the Elmira Project, for instance, occasionally stayed on the computer for as long as forty-five minutes, the length of the free-play period. That was particularly true when they had developed their own game with a partner.

## GAME PROGRAMS

It is important in the beginning to select a program that the children can use with ease; one that they can learn how to use on their own. The choice depends upon your knowledge of the programs available and your objectives for the children. There are any number of good programs available (see chapter 10).

After previewing many programs, we chose *Jeepers Creatures* for our initial program in the Elmira Project because it seemed to satisfy our initial objectives for the children. Another program might have been just as satisfactory. Whatever program you choose for your own children should be based, first of all, on your personal preview of the program. Nevertheless, it is difficult for adults to predict how children will respond to a particular program until they actually use it. The University of Maryland's Computer Discovery Project found that young children were consistently more capable than experienced teachers predicted they would be (Wright and Schwartz 1984).

In this chapter and those to follow, we will describe one or more programs as examples to illustrate what can be used successfully with preliterate children for each of the chapter topics. For this chapter, "The Computer as a Playmate," almost any of the programs we used could serve as examples because preschool children treat them all as games. We will describe only our first program, *Jeepers Creatures*, because it is a good example of a program to use at the beginning.

It is important to consider your objectives when selecting programs. We wanted a program that would fulfill the following objectives:

1. Involve children in a simple but interesting learning game

2. Have simple, nonverbal directions

3. Allow children to learn how to play on their own without difficulty

4. Have a graphic appear on the screen for any key pressed

5. Be a first step in a sequence of programs, each of which would develop skills learned in the previous program.

*Jeepers Creatures* is a mix-and-match animal game that shows a picture of an animal divided into three parts horizontally with its head at the top, its body in the middle, and its feet at the bottom. The three parts are controlled by particular rows of keys on the computer keyboard. The head is controlled by the top row of letter keys (i.e., each letter key will make the head of a different animal appear), the body by the middle row, and the feet by the bottom row of keys. A child can press any letter key and something will happen; that is, the head, the body, or the feet of the animal, along with corresponding background color, will change. Thus, children can mix up heads and bodies and feet of animals, such as the kangaroo, panda bear, octopus, cat, dog, monkey, fish, or owl. Altogether there are three different zoos of ten animals.

If children press three keys in a row vertically, they will get one whole animal on the screen with a monochromatic background. Otherwise, a mixed-up animal will appear with a funny, mixed-up name under it, for example, catowlroo for an animal with the head of a cat, the body of an owl, and the feet of a kangaroo. In addition, the program has a monotonic sound cue for every key pressed. The tone is high- or low-pitched, depending on whether a top, bottom, or middle key is pressed. When three vertical keys are pressed to make a whole animal, a little song plays as a reward or cue that the child has completed the exercise correctly.

To change to a new zoo of ten animals, the child must press the RETURN key. Pressing the space bar makes a surprise animal appear. Pressing the RESET key makes the program start over. The program starts by running through a zoo of ten animals and showing all of their parts. When that is finished, an animal graphic appears on the monitor with the words PRESS ANY KEY in bubble letters (the only written directions). That is the signal for the children to start the game.

## Children's First Experience

At the outset, the children do not know what to do. After they place the program disk into the disk drive and turn on the monitor and computer, the program *Jeepers Creatures* begins running through its zoo. The words PRESS ANY KEY have no meaning for preliterate children at first. After a while, however, they come to recognize this cue at the beginning of any program as their signal to begin.

But what should they do? We observed that many children were hesitant on their first try, even though they had pushed keys without hesitation on the typewriter. Most children eventually started by pressing some of the letter keys on the bottom row. Those who pressed one key and then looked up at the monitor screen were the quickest to figure out the rules of the program. Those who pressed one key after another without looking up did not understand at first that one key controls what happens on the screen. With two children at the keyboard, however, a great deal of peer teaching occurred.

In the beginning, the children pressed only the letters on the bottom row, thereby changing only the feet of the animal. Eventually they learned to press letter keys on the middle and top rows. Then someone discovered that pressing three keys in a row vertically produced one complete animal on the screen. Some children shared this information. Others made it their own special skill, exclaiming: "Look what I can do!"

The children from the four-year-old class had a marvelous time exclaiming over and laughing at the funny animals they had created. They pointed to the screen and touched it. Soon they were making up their own nonsensical names for the animals. As soon as they had mastered the program, they went on to create their own games. Some children made sounds for the animals when it was their turn at the keyboard. Others pushed keys according to rules they had invented. One girl, for instance, said: "I want to push B because that's in my name." She also picked out J because that

*Children can learn to turn on the computer by themselves.*

was in one of the other children's names. One child spent most of his turn trying to sound out the nonsense names at the bottom of each picture, even though he didn't read yet!

Most of the four year olds could spell their own names by the time of the Elmira Project, which took place at the end of the school year. However, only five children from the three-year-old class were able to do so, although a number of them knew one or two letters in their names.

The three year olds approached the computer less exuberantly and were more subdued and had more of a sense of awe. It took them longer to understand what was happening, but once they had induced the rules, they became as expert as the four year olds.

By the second day, several of the children had discovered the surprise animal that appeared when the space bar was pressed. Then others found out how to make a whole animal, although they sometimes forgot exactly which three keys they had pressed when they tried to make the animal again.

Four-year-olds Brian and Mike pressed the RESET button by mistake, starting the program over again. At first they thought they had broken something. However, when they discovered they could not continue playing until the original zoo went through its whole introduction of ten animals again, they were bored. Most of the children, in fact, lost interest when they were not able to make something happen right away. Afterwards, Mike went over to some children at a nearby table and told them: "Whatever you do, don't hit that button because you have to wait for the whole zoo before you can play again."

On the other hand, three-year-old Larson found the RESET button to be a whole new game for him. He pushed it every chance he got and then watched with delight while the ten-animal zoo went through its changes. His partner, Kelly, wanted to get on with the original game and tried to keep Larson from pressing the RESET key, located on the right side of the keyboard, by having him sit in the left-hand chair.

## CHILDREN'S STAGES IN USING COMPUTER GAMES

Children seem to progress through a sequence of observable stages while teaching themselves to use computer games, just as they do when naturally and spontaneously learning to draw, write, build with blocks, and accomplish many other preschool skills (see Chapter 2). At first, we were excited to observe some children making up their own games while using a commercial computer program. Then, we noted that most of the children eventually arrived at this point with each of the programs they learned to use on their own. Finally, we observed the children from start to finish on many new programs and decided they were all following what we have come to call the natural stages of learning through discovery, or the three M's. Wright and Samaras (1986, 75) have also noted a similar play sequence.

There seem to be three stages: manipulation, mastery, and meaning. Watch your own children as they learn by themselves to play computer games and see if you can recognize which stage they are in.

## Manipulation

Children start by physically manipulating the medium to find out what it does and what they can do with it. Using a paintbrush for the first time, a child will swish paint across the paper, often covering one color with another just to see what it is like. Using unit blocks for the first time, a child may fill containers with the blocks and then dump them out repeatedly.

With computer games, children often play with the keys to see what they feel like. "Piano-playing the keyboard" is the term often used. If they happen to bring up a graphic (a computer picture) that they particularly like, they may press the same key over and over. Sometimes during manipulation children will stumble upon the real rules for the game. If they recognize their discovery, they may abandon their "fooling around" and play the game the way it is supposed to be played.

A child often completes the manipulation stage before his or her partner. That child usually shares discoveries about how the game works in order to get on with it. If the other partner doesn't comply and still wants to manipulate, the first child may try to dominate the keyboard or may wait for another more cooperative partner.

## Mastery

The second stage is mastery. Children learn how the program works and play it repeatedly, either alone or with a partner. Once they have mastered the game, they may teach others who show interest. There is a lot of peer teaching by children who have reached mastery.

Invariably the game "experts" invent a new way to use a graphic, press a key, or touch the monitor. Those children reached the next stage, meaning.

## Meaning

It is fascinating to watch children create new uses for each computer game they learn to play. Partners often play the invented game with as much relish as they do the real program. Many of the invented games spread through the entire class. What prompts this creativity? Why does every computer program lead children in the end to invent their own games?

What we witnessed in the Elmira Project is a marvelous illustration of Swiss psychologist Jean Piaget's "symbolic representation." When children master a concept or skill they give meaning to it through symbolic play. Children who have mastered blockbuilding, for instance, build representational buildings. Children who have mastered art skills paint pictures of people and things. Children who have mastered a computer program create new games incorporating the ideas they have learned. They are translating abstract learning into real meaning for themselves. What an exciting discovery—for them and us!

We noted the following invented games for *Jeepers Creatures*:

1. Push a key that is a letter in your name and see what animal appears

2. Make up your own names for the animals you create

3. Make sounds for the animals you create

4. Guess which animal graphic will appear next

5. Sound out the funny names that appear under each animal

6. Name the animals as they appear

## WHAT CHILDREN LEARNED FROM JEEPERS CREATURES

Most of the children in the Elmira Project learned one or more of the following:

1. How to turn the computer and monitor on and off

2. How to hold the program disk, insert it into the disk drive, and extract it when finished

3. How to take turns

4. How to operate the program

5. New vocabulary words (names of animals)

6. The meanings of symbols

7. Self-confidence

You can determine whether children are learning the computer by inviting each of them to teach you how to use it to play *Jeepers Creatures*.

(If you know how, pretend that you don't. Children understand pretending because they do it themselves.) If a child can show you or explain to you what to do, then you will know that he or she understands how to operate the machine and the rules of the game.

## INTEGRATING JEEPERS CREATURES INTO THE CURRICULUM

We chose this particular program not only for its ease of operation by the children, but also for its ease of integration into the preschool curriculum. Selected computer programs should have counterparts and follow-ups in other activity areas. If the children are to learn cognitive concepts, new ideas, new vocabulary, better eye-hand coordination, and other skills from the programs, then they need to be able to practice these skills with similar activities elsewhere in the classroom.

You may find it helpful to introduce the computer program by bringing in a new classroom activity. Ideas for such activities follow each of the computer programs described in this book. You are also encouraged to invent your own introductory activities and follow-up games. Let the computer be a stimulus for all sorts of new experiences. You may also want the children themselves to be involved in the creation of new games.

## ACTIVITIES TO BE USED WITH JEEPERS CREATURES

Several activities will enhance children's experiences with the computer. Those include mix-and-match games, puzzles, animal books, and turn-taking books.

### Mix-and-Match Animal Games

Make your own game by coloring and cutting out ten large animals from a child's coloring book. Mount each animal on a differently colored piece of construction paper. Laminate or cover each animal card with clear contact paper. Cut each card horizontally into thirds with the head in the top third, the body in the middle, and the feet at the bottom. Mix up the cards and put them on a table or the floor in the manipulative area.

Observe which children get the idea of arranging the cards to make one whole animal. Don't be tempted to direct the children. They will probably make up their own games with the cards. Does any child try to put three different cards together to make a ''crazy animal''? Do any children make up funny names for the animals they create? This activity, an excellent introduction to *Jeepers Creatures,* should be kept in a clear plastic box on your puzzle shelf where it is easily accessible to the children.

## Animal Puzzles

This is the time to have animal puzzles available on your manipulative shelves and tables.

## Strange Animal Books

Joanne and David Wyle's *A Funny Fish Story* (Children's Press, 1984) is a marvelously simple and funny story that converts colorful pictures of a dog to a dogfish, a cat to a catfish, a cow to a cowfish, and so forth. Children should make the connection with *Jeepers Creatures* without any trouble.

Leo Lionni's *Fish Is Fish* (New York: Pantheon Books, 1970) is a similar but more complicated story of a fish that misses its tadpole friend after it becomes a frog. The frog returns to the pond to describe to the fish (in wonderful illustrations) all the fascinating creatures on land, which all take on a decidedly fishy look.

Let the children make up their own strange animal stories.

## Turn-Taking Books

Because this is your children's first experience on the computer, they may have trouble taking turns initially. A story about turn taking may help. Try reading Dorothy Corey's *Everybody Takes a Turn* (Chicago: Albert Whitman and Co., 1980). It is a book of pictures showing first one child and then another taking a turn with something.

A much funnier book is *Your Turn, Doctor* by Carla Perez and Deborah Robison (New York: Dial Books for Young Readers, 1982). When Gloria goes to the doctor for her checkup, she becomes the examiner and makes the doctor go through the uncomfortable but hilarious indignities of a checkup.

## ARCADE GAME PROGRAMS

Many of the arcade computer games are too advanced for the preschooler. Even those that are not may be inappropriate. First, most arcade games promote winning, which also means that someone loses. This type of competition does not have a place in the preschool program. Young children should be concerned with developing their skills to the best of their ability, not trying to win a game—and especially not trying to defeat someone else.

Second, arcade games that shoot down, blow up, or destroy people, animals, inanimate objects, space ships, and cities should not be allowed in the preschool classroom. Many arcade games feature sophisticated weapons of destruction. Most preschools do not allow guns or military toys in their programs; they also should restrict the use of computer games that shoot or blow up things.

Children treat all computer programs as games. Therefore, you need not look for an arcade-type program in order to have a game. If you carefully preview and select appropriate programs, then your children will learn not only the concepts and skills involved, but also the values they should espouse.

## OBSERVING CHILDREN USING GAME PROGRAMS

One of the things that we as early childhood educators often lack is the opportunity to observe closely the individual children we teach. While they are engaged in various activities, often rushing from one to the other, we are engaged in directing group activities or responding to an individual's request (and never the twain shall meet). Thus, we miss in important information-gathering opportunity. We think we know our children because we are with them every day. But do we? Have we really stepped back and taken an objective look at every child? Many educators agree that nothing can take the place of observing individual children.

Using the computer in the classroom affords that opportunity. If you spend no more than ten minutes of your time every day to observe one child at the computer, you can glean invaluable information about him or her. The child is stationary and engaged in a compelling activity. You will be able to observe him or her without being noticed by positioning yourself some distance behind the child.

What should you look for? With early game programs you may be concerned with an individual child's development of social skills. How does the child interact with his or her partner? Narrative recording is usually best for observing individual children, and you may want to consider the following questions:

1. Does the child wait for a turn?

2. Does the child take turns without a fuss?

3. Does the child control the turn at the computer?

4. Does the child interact with the partner? How?

5. Does the child give information or help? What?

6. Is the child's partner a friend?

7. What is the relationship between child and partner during other classroom activities?

On the other hand, you may want to know how each child is progressing through the stages of learning. Is the child still manipulating the keys? Has he or she mastered the program? What kinds of new games has the child invented?

The opportunity for individual child observation has not been viewed as a reason for incorporating the computer into the early childhood classroom. Researchers observe young children on computers during their studies, but what about the classroom staff? Here is an unparalleled opportunity to see how children learn through play; to observe how the discovery method really works; to determine where each child stands in his or her development. The chapters to follow will encourage such observation and offer guidelines about what to look for.

# REFERENCES

Barnes, B. J., and S. Hill. "Should Young Children Work with Microcomputers—Logo before Lego?" *The Computing Teacher* 10 (1986), 11–14.

Beaty, Janice J., and W. Hugh Tucker. *Becoming Partners with a Computer: Preschoolers Learn How.* 1985. Elmira, N.Y.: 3-to-5, P.O. Box 3213, 14905. Videotape.

Beaty, Janice J., and Hugh Tucker. *Computer in the Preschool: An Integrated Activity.* 1985. Elmira, N.Y.: 3-to-5, P.O.Box 3213, 14905. Slides and Tape.

Borgh, Karin, and W. Patrick Dickson. "Two Preschoolers Sharing One Microcomputer: How They Handle It." In *Young Children and Microcomputers,* edited by Patricia Campbell and Greta Fein. Englewood Cliffs, N.J.: Prentice-Hall, 1986.

Isenberg, Joan, and Marianne Latall. "Microcomputers in a Developmentally Based Preschool Program: Assets or Liabilities. Paper presented at the National Association for the Education of Young Children Conference, Los Angeles, November 1984.

Jewson, Jan, and Roy D. Pea. "*Logo* Research at Bank Street College." *BYTE* 7 (1982), 332–33.

Kimmel, Stephen. "Programs for Preschoolers: Starting Out Young." *Creative Computing,* (October 1983): 44–45.

Lipinski, Judith M., Robert E. Nida, Daniel D. Shade, and J. Allen Watson. *Competence, Gender and Preschooler's Free Play Choices When a Microcomputer Is Present in the Classroom.* ERIC Document, ED 243 609, 1984.

Murphy, Brian J. "Educational Programs for the Very Young." *Creative Computing,* (October 1983): 107–18.

Niebor, Ruth Ann. *A Study of the Effect of Computers on the Preschool Environment.* ERIC Document, ED 234 898, 1983.

Shade, Daniel, Gloria E. Daniel, Robert E. Nida, Judith M. Lipinski, and J. Allen Watson. *Microcomputers: A Close Look at What Happens When Preschool Children Interact with Age-Appropriate Software.* ERIC Document, ED 243 608, 1983.

Sheingold, K. "Issues Related to the Implementation of Computer Technology in Schools: A Cross-Section Study." Paper presented at The National Institute Related to the Implementation of Computer Technology in Schools, Washington, D.C., February 1981.

Sweetnam, George. "Computer Kids, the 21st Century Elite." *Science Digest,* (November 1982), 85–88.

Watt, Dan. "*Logo* in the Schools." *BYTE* 7 (1982), 116–34.

————. "Games designed for Learning." *Popular Computing,* (July 1983): 65–67.

Wright, June L., and Anastacia S. Samaras. "Play Worlds and Microworlds." In *Young Children and Microcomputers,* edited by Patricia F. Campbell and Greta G. Fein. Englewood Cliffs, N.J.: Prentice-Hall, 1986.

Wright, June L., and Shirley Schwartz. "Researching the Microcomputer as an Integral Part of the Preschool Curriculum." Paper presented at the National Association for the Education of Young Children Conference, Los Angeles, November 1984.

# SOFTWARE

*Creature Creator*
> Design Ware
> 185 Berry St.
> San Francisco, Calif. 94017

Apple, DOS 3.3, 48K

This program allows users to create creatures from a selection of heads, bodies, arms, and legs. Dance sequences can then be designed for the creatures to perform. A game allows users to match a creature's dance steps to a pattern. (Grades preschool–3)

**"Creature Features" from the program *Alphabet Beasts and Co.***
> Software Productions
> 2357 Southway Drive
> P.O. Box 21341
> Columbus, Ohio 43221

Apple II series, DOS 3.3, 48K; Commodore 64; IBM PC, PCjr.; disk.

Children can create fantasy beasts to help them with letter and number recognition skills. In "Creature Features" there are 256 combinations of body parts belonging to a dragon, alien, genie, and boy.

*Jeepers Creatures*
>Kangaroo, Inc.
>110 S. Michigan Ave., Suite 469
>Chicago, Ill. 60605

Apple II series; Atari
(Discussed in chapter)

**Mix and Match**
>Apple Computer, Inc.
>20525 Mariani Ave.
>Cupertino, Calif. 95104

Apple II series, high-resolution graphics; 1981
Sesame Street Muppets are featured in four different game programs. In *Mix and Match* the operator follows directions at the bottom of the screen to make a new Muppet from parts of old ones. The new Muppet is then given a mixed-up name. Preschoolers can learn to follow directions.

**Monster Chase**
>Basics and Beyond
>Pinesbridge Rd.
>P.O. Box 10
>Amawalk, N.Y., 10501

TRS–80 Model I, III, 4
This is a program that introduces the young child to computing.

## LEARNING ACTIVITIES

1. Create a game, such as the mix-and-match animal game described on page 48, and use it with your children as an introduction to a computer program. Record the results.
2. Observe different partners as they use the computer on three different days. Record how they work out turn taking and any peer teaching that takes place.
3. Make a list of your children who are using a particular computer game and try to determine by observation their learning stage.
4. Observe and record all of the creative ways your children have invented to use on the computer programs they are familiar with.
5. Make a list of all of the learning and developmental growth you have noted in your children since they started using the computer. Look for things like new vocabulary, cognitive concepts, eye-hand coordination, turn-taking skills, and so forth. Give the evidence you observed for each item on your list.

Chapter 4

# The Computer as an Alphabet Book

**W**hen young children first meet letters, they like to play around with them, just as they play with blocks or clay. They may be familiar with the names of some, but they still like to explore their qualities by naming them, finding them in the alphabet, and touching them, just as they do with any new object. Letters have no intrinsic meaning to young children at first. Young children do not realize that letters and words tell the story in a picture book. In fact, preliterate children tend to think the story is conveyed by the pictures in the book (Vukelich and Golden 1984, 4).

Children's recognition of letters often has to do with their problem of distinguishing writing from drawing (Ferreiro and Teberosky 1979, 35). Because their own first drawing and writing attempts are usually scribbles, they begin to identify writing as linear scribbles. Their first printed letter is often the initial letter of their first name. To children this letter seems to convey the entire meaning of their name, and they may not pay much attention to the remaining letters.

Other letters are recognized on the basis of use. Besides those in their own names, children recognize letters they see repeatedly on TV, in stores, on T-shirts, on toys. One of the least used English letters is the letter *Z*. Yet, preliterate children who have seen the TV cartoon Zorro easily recognize *Z* before a more commonly used letter, for instance, *E* (Ferreiro and Teberosky, 40).

Children's first printed letters are often written all over the page rather than in a horizontal line. They also print letters upside down and sideways. For example, most children go through a reversal phase of printing all the letters backwards. Consequently, they have trouble recognizing some letters, such as *W*, which appears to be an upside down *M*.

Children need to learn by trying out letters playfully in all sorts of situations that there is a particular way each letter is written and a particular direction each should face. They need to discover the rules about letters just as they discover the rules about speaking English—on their own.

55

To help children learn what letters are about, preschool programs should provide letter activities, such as alphabet blocks and magnetic letters. Teachers should print children's names on their art products; they'll soon find the children trying their own hand at it. Children need to see letters on labels posted around the room—*housekeeping*, *library*, *blocks*—although they may not understand what the words mean at first. They should see teachers writing and printing letters. When children are surrounded by letters, they will want to know about letters and use them.

Because children learn about letters through playful exploration, preschool teachers who try to teach them the alphabet formally are wasting their time. Of course, the children will learn to chant in rote, but seldom will the concepts become really meaningful.

## THE ALPHABET

Nevertheless, children should learn the alphabet, shouldn't they? It's important because of the many alphabet books and computer alphabet programs on the market, isn't it? Not necessarily. Surprising as it may seem to the lay person, the alphabet is not the first thing preliterate children need to learn about letters. To learn the twenty-six letters of the English alphabet in sequence is superfluous for children who don't yet need them. In fact, children do not really learn letters in a meaningful way until they begin to use them.

At the very least, children should learn the alphabet before learning to write, shouldn't they? Not really. Studies have shown that "young children learn to write through a process that is really quite the opposite. Rather than learning to write by mastering first the parts (letters) and then building up to the whole (written lines), it appears that children first attend to the whole and only much later to the parts" (Temple 1982, 19).

Most preschoolers can recite the alphabet by rote in the words of a chant or song: *A–B–C–D–E–F–G–H–I–J–K–elemenopee*. However, they are not necessarily able to separate the individual letters in the song. They believe *elemenopee* is all one word! They will not truly have the need for learning the entire alphabet in its order until they have to alphabetize or to index.

Many authors of picture books and developers of computer programs, nevertheless, assume the alphabet is the first thing that toddlers and preschoolers should learn. Hence, there is a continuous flood of alphabet books and computer alphabet programs. Parents have no reason to doubt the publishers of such books and programs. They also believe that in order to learn to read, the first thing a child needs to know is the alphabet.

Montessori preschool programs, renowned for their promotion of early reading in children, do not stress learning the alphabet in sequence. They introduce letters to children very early, but they begin with the first letters children use themselves; for example, *m*. Further, they teach children the letter sound, *m–mmmmm*, rather than the letter name, *em*.

Preliterate children do need to recognize certain letters, for instance, those in their own names and other important words they might encounter. However, they do not need to learn all twenty-six at once. Learning a few letters consistently is more important for three and four year olds than reciting the alphabet.

Young children do need to learn the names or sounds for the letters, and they do need to recognize letter symbols before they can progress in writing and reading. However, they do not need to recognize, identify, and use the entire alphabet at first.

## THE COMPUTER AS AN ALPHABET BOOK

Which letters, then, should children be exposed to, and how can they learn them? Both questions can be answered in the same manner. Children should be able to choose out of the whole alphabet the particular letters they need to use, and they should be able to learn them on their own by playing around with them. That is what makes computer alphabet programs powerful. Because alphabet programs contain all the letters and allow children to play around with them, they encourage young children to select what they need from the alphabet and learn it in a pleasurable and meaningful manner.

Rather an expensive alphabet book, you might at first decide. Yet, the computer is much more than a book. Computer programs are interactive, never passive. Children manipulate the computer and the program responds. They discover by trial and error or by just plain guessing. Then they play the program until they have mastered the concepts. Finally, they make the concepts meaningful by creating their own games. All of these learning steps are tailored to the individual needs of children because they do them on their own.

## STICKYBEAR ABC

*Stickybear ABC* is an alphabet program that fulfills the five objectives for children listed on page 42. It is a high-resolution-graphic program in which the child presses a letter to bring up one of two animated/sound graphics that illustrate the letter. The name of the graphic appears at the top of the screen and the uppercase letter appears at the bottom. The following graphics are included:

> A  = airplane flying
>      apple falling off a tree

B  = bee buzzing around Stickybear's head
     bouncing ball

C  = piece of cake on a table and Stickybear sneaking up
     Stickybear crying with tears falling

D  = duck quacking and swimming
     door opening and closing after knocking sound

E  = elephants moving trunks to the tune of "Baby Elephant Walk"
     egg bouncing and breaking

F  = fish swimming
     flowers bursting into bloom

G  = grass growing upward to cover the screen
     grapes on a table as Stickybear rises up from behind

H  = helicopter flying around a mountain
     hat flying through the air

I  = tropical island with a cloud moving to the tune "Aloha Oe"
     Stickybear eating an ice-cream cone

J  = juggler juggling balls
     Stickybear jumping over a mound

K  = kite in the air with tail waving
     Stickybear Mama and Papa kissing

L  = lamp going on and off
     ladder with Stickybear going up and down

M  = mountain with floating cloud
     moon blinking in the night sky

N  = night sky with stars and the tune "Twinkle, Twinkle"
     needle sewing

O  = octopus doing a dance
     orange bouncing

P  = penquin popping out of the water
     parrot standing and flapping its wings

Q  = quilt over Stickybear lying on the bed
     queen walking across the room

R  = rabbit hopping
     rain falling

S  = sailboat with moving cloud and the tune "Sailing, Sailing
       snow falling

T  = television with Stickybear performing
       train moving

U  = umbrella over Stickybear's head as he walks along
       underwear on Stickybear

V  = vegetables on a table as Stickybear rises up from behind
       volcano with bubbling top

W = Stickybear blowing a whistle
       windmill going around

X  = X-ray of Stickybear's ribs turning on and off
       xylophone playing

Y  = yo-yo going up and down
       yellow color filling the screen

Z  = zebra moving
       zipper opening and closing


    To operate the program on an Apple II computer, the children in-
sert the disk, turn on the monitor and computer, and wait for the bubble
letters PRESS ANY LETTER to appear on the title. This is the only written
instruction. On the Commodore 64 the child must first load the program by
typing in LOAD "PRG",8,1. This command is used on the Commodore to
load the entire Stickybear series of programs. It normally takes a four year
old about two sessions to learn this command. On both Apple and Commodore
a letter graphic appears whenever a letter is pressed. The accompanying
animation and sound continue until they are stopped by pressing another
letter. Only letters are used in this program. Pressing any other key has no
effect.

    The Commodore version of *Stickybear ABC* has two other alphabet
games that do not appear on the Apple version. Pressing the F3 function
key plays the "Match Game." In the "Match Game" the entire alphabet
appears on the screen with one letter in a different color. When the child
presses the matching key on the keyboard, related pictures appear on the
screen. A second game is an order game in which the children must press
each letter of the alphabet in order. If the wrong letter is pressed, the program makes a chirping noise and shows the alphabet with the proper letter
highlighted. Only the Apple version of *Stickybear ABC* was used in the Elmira
Project.

*Stickybear ABC* was chosen because it appealed to children through its vibrantly colored high-resolution graphics and Stickybear characters. The entier *Stickybear* preschool series was chosen for this appeal and for ease of operation by preliterate children. Each program in the series operated in a slightly different manner from every other program, each being slightly more advanced than the one before. Thus, we were able to introduce in a stepwise fashion increasingly difficult preschool programs.

## INTRODUCING THE PROGRAM

During circle time the teacher focused on letters, asking individuals what letter their names started with. She also read *The Strawberry Look Book* that accompanied the program. The story introduced Papa, Mama, and Boy Stickybear. It consisted of a colorful picture book with one sentence of text at the top of the page and each item labeled in the supermarket, toy store, clothing store, restaurant, furniture store, bakery, florist, and garage that the bears visit.

*The Strawberry Look Book* requires that individuals or small groups sit close to the teacher in order to see the items on the page. The listeners may want to tell the story themselves because the text contains no plot. Preliterate children will probably not be able to read the labels on each object but should not find it difficult to identify the food, clothing, and furniture items. Such a book illustrates the concept that every object has a name that can be written with letters. Each of the computer graphics in the program also has a written name and an alphabet letter to represent it.

The teacher also tried to use the accompanying *Stickybear ABC* poster to introduce the program. The poster contained all of the graphics from the program. It seemed confusing to the children because so much detailed information was illustrated. We found this particular poster made more sense to the children after they were familiar with the program. It was, in fact, an excellent follow-up. We posted it on the wall near the computer where children could make the connection between the graphics on the monitor and those on the poster.

Did the children look at the poster and make the connection? We had no evidence that such was the case until the second week. One child who liked to dominate her turn at the computer turned to her partner and, pointing at the poster, ordered: "You go use the other computer, and I am using this one." Her partner then got up and moved her chair over to the poster!

## STAGES IN USING ALPHABET PROGRAMS

As with other learning experiences, children go through three stages when learning to use alphabet programs. Those stages of manipulation, mastery, and meaning are described below.

### Manipulation

The children were delighted with the new program. Stickybear and his world looked fascinating. Experienced operators began by pushing one key at a time and waiting to see what would happen. Children with little experience on the computer began by "piano-playing" the keys. Their partners soon told them to press one key at a time. Nevertheless, few of the children realized at first that each letter key controlled a different graphic. They were used to *Jeepers Creatures* in which they pushed letters randomly by row.

Most children overgeneralized the rules learned from the first program. They pressed any letter key, just as they had learned to do with *Jeepers Creatures*, but they did not know at first how to make a particular graphic reappear. In addition, several of the children sat and waited for something to happen at the beginning of the program, instead of pressing keys when prompted by the words PRESS ANY LETTER. They were used to watching the zoo go through its lengthy paces in *Jeepers Creatures* and assumed that all computer programs had a similar introduction.

Overgeneralization is, in fact, how children learn most new concepts. They tend to apply the rules they have already learned to every similar situation. A classic example concerns the English language rule in which the past tense for regular verbs is formed by adding *ed*. Young children in the process of acquiring the English language overgeneralize by applying this ending to all verbs, saying, for example, "I runned" or "Mama bringed the milk."

The lessons taught by *Stickybear ABC* were more sophisticated than those taught by *Jeepers Creatures*. The children had to learn not only that each letter controlled two different graphics, but also that they could call up a particular graphic if they knew what letter it started with and where to find the letter on the keyboard. Chris did not know the letter Q at first, but his partner Aaron did. Before his time at the keyboard was over, Chris had mastered Q and several other new letters.

There was a pronounced difference between children who knew their alphabet letters and those who did not. The former extracted more variety from the program. But, because one of the partners usually was more advanced than the other, learning new letters constantly took place by peer teaching.

## Mastery

Mastery requires time. Children need to play together without a break for as long as possible if they are to understand the unstated rules of a program. Such a practice was possible in the Elmira Project because so many other interesting activities were available in the classroom. The children did not seem to be disappointed when they could not immediately use the computer during free-play time. They were content to participate in other activities while waiting for a turn. Partners were able to experiment with programs for ten minutes or more every day.

Frequently, one partner would be ready to move on to another activity before the other partner was. In that event, he or she simply found another child who was ready and willing to wear the computer necklace. The remaining partner at the keyboard then had the opportunity to teach the new partner how to operate the program. Peer teaching reinforced the child's learning while strengthening verbal abilities and interpersonal skills. A true test of learning requires that the learner be able to teach the newly acquired skill to someone else.

Children soon learned to control the program and began to press letters that brought up their favorite graphics. The four year olds laughed uproariously and covered their faces with their hands when a new graphic

*Children soon learn to press the proper key to find their favorite graphic.*

appeared on the screen. The yo-yo was a favorite, perhaps because of the funny sound it made as it went up and down. One of the girls learned about K, for kiss, right away. Then she whispered to her next partner, "push K." Both dissolved into giggles when the Stickybears kissed. One of the boys was fascinated by watching the grass grow in the graphic for G. He pushed G several times to watch the grass grow.

## Meaning

The experienced children quickly arrived at the meaning stage with this program. Once they had mastered the program's operation, they acquired meaning by inventing their own games. Because there were so many highly animated graphics, the children made up more games than they had with *Jeepers Creatures*. The simplest game was to trace the letter on the screen with a finger, much as children do with sandpaper letters.

A more complicated game evolved from the children's discovery that pressing any letter would stop the animation on the screen. Many children discovered this fact on their own, but others passed along the information and taught their partner their own version of the "I Caught You" or "I Stopped You" game they had invented. The idea was to stop the graphic by pressing a key before something happened. For instance, in the island graphic, the children tried to stop the cloud from reaching the palm tree. In the egg graphic, one child tried to stop the egg as it bounced, before it broke open. In the Kiss graphic, a child would try to stop the animation before the two Stickybears kissed.

One partner would press the particular letter to bring up the animated graphic on the screen. The other would try to press a key to stop the animation just at the right time. Conversation from several taped sessions went as follows: "I pushed it. Now it's your turn." "I stopped you. I stopped you." "I'm going to catch you." "I caught you." "You didn't catch me." "You caught me kissing." "I'm catching you." "Are you going to do it? Oh, you missed. Now you've got to wait." (Here the child had to push E twice to get back to the bouncing egg). "E, elephant. E is for egg."

Another favorite game invented by the children was touching the screen for certain graphics. Children tried to put their hand over the buzzing bee in the bee graphic, to open the door for Stickybear in the door graphic, to grab the piece of cake in the cake graphic so that Stickybear wouldn't get it. One study of four year olds and the computer also used the *Stickybear* series. For the *ABC* program it was reported that some children knocked on the door when it appeared on the screen and kissed the two Stickybears when they appeared in the kiss graphic. (Shade 1983, 14). Touching the monitor seemed to make the children a part of what was happening in the graphic, yet it was not destructive to the equipment.

*These children are playing a game they invented for an alphabet program.*

Other games invented by children who had mastered the program in the Elmira Project included pushing the power light on the keyboard, pretending it was hot, and then laughing. Mike and Scott tried to match the pictures on the Stickybear poster to the graphics that appeared on the monitor; therefore, it is important for teachers to mount such posters as close as possible to the computer. Other children tried their skill at naming the letters and objects as they appeared, for example h for hat or h for helicopter.

## WHAT CHILDREN LEARNED FROM STICKYBEAR ABC

Children continued the self-learning they had begun with *Jeepers Creatures* and extended it to include new cognitive concepts, manipulative skills, language skills, and computer skills, including:

1. Location of the various letters on the keyboard
2. Cause and effect (namely, that one key caused two different graphics to appear)

3. Which letters controlled which graphic

4. How to press a key quickly enough to stop the animation

5. New alphabet letters

6. Many new vocabulary words (for example, volcano, juggler, penguin)

7. The rules for the new program

The adult observers were impressed with how quickly and how far the children could go on their own with a new program in just a few days. In the beginning, most children experimented with the keys to see what happened when they pressed each one. At first, they concentrated more on the keys than on the monitor, thereby missing the cause-and-effect lesson being illustrated on the screen. Then, they became excited about the funny graphics, animation, and sound. While the four year olds laughed out loud, the three year olds stared as if in a trance. Finally, they made the connection between the key being pressed and the graphic that appeared. It was a breakthrough in understanding for the children, but the real thrill seemed to be their own control over what happened in the program.

A fascinating event happened during the third week when Larson's 1½-year-old brother came to visit. Because he wanted to sit at the computer like the other children, the teacher showed him how to use his computer finger and let him try it. He started like the experienced operators by pressing one key at a time and watching the screen to see what happened. Although he did not try to identify the letters on the keys or the monitor, he did name many of the graphics!

## ACTIVITIES TO BE USED WITH COMPUTER ALPHABET PROGRAMS

Activities that can be used to enhance alphabet programs are limitless. Some of those are described below.

### Alphabet Letters in Fun Activities

Keep several games and activities with alphabet letters on the shelves in your manipulative area. You can make or purchase cardboard-mounted sandpaper letters for the children to touch and feel. Be sure the front is distinguishable from the back so that children will learn the correct orientation of the letter.

Any kind of three-dimensional letter can be played with or traced; children love to trace around letters that are large enough. A parent with a jig saw can make an entire wooden alphabet of three-dimensional letters for the class, or it can be purchased commercially. To make another game for the children, trace the outlines of these letters on white posterboard and let the children try to match each letter to its tracing. Hollow plastic letters can be purchased and used as molds for making sand letters. Magnetic letters are also fun.

Another alphabet-matching game for more experienced preschoolers can be made from a paperback alphabet book that the teacher cuts out and laminates with clear self-adhesive paper. The letters should be cut apart from the objects to let the children try to match them. Books with one simple picture representing each letter of the alphabet are best. Keep such puzzles and matching games in separate manila envelopes with a picture label of each.

Remember, these should be activities that the children play with, not lessons that you formally teach them.

## Pretzel Letters

Have pretzels for snacks occasionally and let children see how many different letters they can create by breaking the pretzels. This is a good follow-up activity to *Stickybear ABC*.

## Alphabet Soup

Have alphabet soup for snack or lunch and see how many letters the children can identify. Better yet, have the children assist in preparing the soup.

## An Alphabet Field Trip

Use *The Strawberry Look Book* as a lead-in for a field trip to a supermarket, a restaurant, a bakery, a florist, or a furniture store. See how many items the children can identify by their first letters.

## A Funny Alphabet Book

Because some preschool children may consider alphabet books too babyish, try using some funny ones to tickle their fancy.

Dennis Nolan's *Alphabrutes* (Englewood Cliffs, N.J.: Prentice-Hall, 1977) is a nearly wordless picture book of weird but friendly green monsters, each with a letter on its T-shirt representing the sound it makes.

Roger Hargreave's *Albert the Alphabetical Elephant* (New York: Grosset and Dunlap Publishers, 1982) is a story of a little girl and a blue elephant who teaches her the alphabet by making lowercase letters with his trunk. The difference between upper- and lowercase letters does not need to be stressed in the preschool, but children should write their own name using both in order to avoid confusion later. A book like this could introduce the concept.

*Dr. Seuss's ABC* (New York: Random House, 1963) carries the upper-lowercase concept further by illustrating it with a strange menagerie of beasts and children.

Robin and Jocelyn Wild's *The Bears' ABC Book* (New York: Harper and Row, 1977) is a wonderfully illustrated book about the fun had by three bears rummaging in a dump and extracting items to create an alphabet of zany playthings. This book should go well with the children's *Stickybear* computer experience.

Mary Elting and Michael Folsom's *Q Is for Duck: An Alphabet Guessing Game* (Clarion Books, 1980) starts out thus: "A is for Zoo. . .why?" It then goes through the entire alphabet asking such questions and answering them with simple text and cartoon-type illustrations. Children who are experienced on the computer should really enjoy this challenge.

## OBSERVING CHILDREN USING ALPHABET PROGRAMS

It is important to know which children are familiar with the alphabet before they start using alphabet computer programs. Ask each one to spell his or her name aloud or in writing. This exercise gives you baseline information about each child. Then, when you observe children using the program, try to ask yourself the following:

1. Do they recognize the letters on the keys?

2. How long does it take them to find a particular key?

3. Do they recognize the letters on the graphics?

4. Can they make the association between the key they press and the graphic that appears?

5. Which letters do they press most often?

6. Which letters do they seldom press?

7. Does one child teach another about the program?

8. What creative letter games do they invent?

You should observe the children as they interact with letter materials in the classroom. Do they play with letter games or avoid them? Do they like alphabet books? Try reading an alphabet book to a child who has worked with an alphabet program and take note of how he or she responds.

## REFERENCES

Beaty, Janice J., and W. Hugh Tucker. *Computer in the Preschool: An Integrated Activity.* 1985. Elmira, N.Y.: 3-to-5, P.O. Box 3213, 14905. Slides and Tape.

Beaty, Janice J. *Observing Development of the Young Child.* Columbus, Ohio: Merrill Publishing Co., 1986.

Chall, Jeanne. *Learning to Read: The Great Debate.* New York: McGraw-Hill, 1967.

Ferreiro, Emilia, and Ana Teberosky. *Literacy Before Schooling* (translated from Spanish). Exeter, N.H.: Heinemann Educational Books, 1979.

Murphy, Brian J. "Educational Programs for the Very Young." *Creative Computing,* (October 1983): 107–18.

Shade, Daniel D., et al. *Microcomputers: A Close Look at What Happens When Preschool Children Interact with Age-Appropriate Software.* ERIC Document, ED 243 608, 1983.

Temple, Charles A., et al. *The Beginnings of Writing.* Boston: Allyn and Bacon, 1982.

Vukelich, Carol, and Joanne Golden. "Early Writing: Development and Teaching Strategies." *Young Children,* (January 1984): 3–8.

## SOFTWARE

*Alphabet*
          Moses Engineering
          P.O. Box 11038
          Huntsville, Ala. 35805
Atari, 16K; TRS-80 Color Computer; Commodore VIC-20, 5K; cassette
Children learn the alphabet through picture presentations. (Preschool)

*Alphabet Beasts and Company*
          Reader's Digest Software
          Microcomputer Division
          Pleasantville, N.Y. 10570
Apple II family, disk; Commodore 64; IBM PC, PCjr; color monitor
Children learn the alphabet and numbers in a picturebook fashion. (Grades preschool–3)

*Alphabet Circus*
          Developmental Learning Materials
          One DLM Park, P.O. Box 4000
          Allen, Tex. 75002
Apple II family
Includes several circus games: "Meet the Circus" explores alphabetical order;

"Lost Letter" is a matching game; "Alphabet Parade" plays the alphabet song, and when it stops, players must supply next letter; "Secret Letters" is a two-player guessing game with an animated ringmaster; "Juggler" tosses up a letter that the child must find and press on the keyboard; "Marquee Maker" has children spell out names and messages. (Grades preschool–2)

*Alphabet Soup: Winnie the Pooh's Alphabet Adventures and Mickey's Lucky Stars*

> NEC Home Electronics (USA), Inc.
> 1401 Estes Ave.
> Elk Grove Village, Ill. 60007–5463

PC-6000

Children learn the alphabet from Winnie the Pooh and by catching falling stars. (Grades preschool–2)

*Alphabet Zoo*

> Spinnaker Software Corp.
> One Kendall Square
> Cambridge, Mass. 02139

Apple II family; Atari 400, 800, XL; Commodore 64; IBM PC N jr.; disk, cassette; high-resolution graphics;

Simple program in which computer draws pictures for letters. Children watch with little control. (Grades preschool–3)

*Kiri's Hodge Podge*

> Dynacomp, Inc.
> 1427 Monroe Ave.
> Rochester, N.Y. 14618

Apple II family, 32K; Atari; TRS-80; cassette, disk

Children can press any letter and a low-resolution graphic will appear that illustrates the letter. Also appearing will be the letter itself and a sound, often the first line of a familiar nursery tune. The illustrations and numbers may be animated (for example, a green worm moves fast for *Q*—quick worm). Several different objects may appear for some letters (for example, goat, horse, cat, pig, cow for *F*—farm).

*Stickybear ABC*

> Weekly Reader Family Software
> A Division of Xerox Education Publications
> Middletown, Conn. 06457

Apple II family, 48K, DOS 3.3; Atari, 48K

Discussed in this chapter. (Grades preschool–1)

# LEARNING ACTIVITIES

1. Have your children help you make name tags or name cards for each of them before they use the computer. Note which children know the letters

and which ones do not. Do a similar letter activity with each child after he or she has used the alphabet program for several weeks. Do you note any differences?

2. Read an alphabet book to individual children before and after they learn to use the alphabet program. How do each child's comments or reactions differ between the first and second reading?

3. Observe and record how nonverbal or shy children use the alphabet program. How does their use of it compare with that of other children?

4. Which children show a strong interest or preference for the alphabet program? What other classroom activities are they interested in?

5. What creative games do your children invent to use with the alphabet program?

# The Computer as an Abacus

I n the beginning there is a great deal of confusion between numbers and letters for young children. Both numbers and letters have graphic symbols that look much alike to nonreading children. Both systems have word names that can be spoken and written. Additionally, both seem to the child to have something to do with reading. Children do not realize at first that the functions of these two systems of symbols are completely different: numbers are for counting and letters are for spelling.

Children first encounter numbers when they are as young as twenty months old, often in the nursery rhymes they chant (Richardson 1980, 252). They begin to identify with numbers when they learn their age. A number comes to mean them personally: they are "two" and they learn to hold up two fingers to prove it.

Children first learn to count with number games, such as *one, two, buckle my shoe.* The names of numbers are no different to children than the names of any other objects. In fact, they are likely to consider the numbers 1 to 10 as one long word, *onetwothreefourfivesixseveneightnineten,* just as they do their chanted alphabet. They do not separate the numbers in their minds and would not be able to point out three or five of anything.

Children next learn to count objects. The order of the numbers is still fuzzy to them and they often leave out one or two numbers. When pointing to separate objects as they count, they may recite more than one number for the same object. Children have not yet developed the concept of one-to-one correspondence; that the number one stands for one object and two for two objects.

Such is the status of most preschool children. They have heard numbers, chanted numbers, held up their fingers for numbers, played with numbers, but they still do not know what numbers mean. Number symbols remind them of letter symbols. After all, look at 0 and O or 1, I and l. How are children to know that two of those are numbers and the others are letters? How are they to comprehend that the name for a letter stands for a sound, but the name for a number means a quantity? How are children to learn what numbers are all about? By now the answer must be obvious: they will learn them by exploring, trying them out, and playing around with them.

## THE COMPUTER AS AN ABACUS

The classroom computer invites children to get involved with numbers, just as it did with letters. Illustrated, animated, sound-filled number programs present number concepts as games, puzzles, or cartoons with which children must interact to discover their meaning. Just as the ancient abacus still serves as a calculating device for shopkeepers and bankers of the Orient, so the contemporary computer stands ready to introduce modern children to the fascinating world of numbers.

If your classroom were to provide such an invitation, would it mean that your children could learn to manipulate numbers without fear of failure; that they might enjoy doing it; that they could escape the math anxiety that hangs heavily over so many lives? If the answer is yes, then acquire a computer for your classroom. Only the future can tell whether our new computer generations will come to treat numbers as symbols that are interesting, informative, and even fun to use.

If math is to end up as fun, then it must begin as fun. Children need to play with numbers, to manipulate them, to master them, and finally to create new uses for them, just as they do with blocks and beads and bubbles—and letters. Number programs seem an ideal way to start. If you have chosen your programs wisely (see chapter 10), then all you need do is to make the disks available during free play, observe what each child does with the programs, and fill your activity areas with follow-up number activities.

## ESSENTIAL NUMBER KNOWLEDGE

What do preschoolers need to know about numbers? They should build on their present knowledge that numbers have names; that they have symbols; that they can be used to count objects. The numbers from 0 to 10 are enough in the beginning. Although many teachers go through the number days of the month with their class every morning, it is doubtful that the children have any real conception of what is meant by the twentieth of December or the seventeenth of May. They may understand more clearly number games with real objects. (Can you bring us five blocks, Orion?)

Although children seem to write letter symbols before they write number symbols, they may be responding to adult priorities. Observers have noted that young children talk about numbers early and may even refer to letters as numbers. On the other hand, they never seem to refer to numbers as letters (Ferreiro and Teberosky 1979, 37). Children usually learn to recognize number symbols before they can actually write them. However, because writing depends on eye-hand coordination as well as cognitive development, teachers should not worry about preschoolers' lack of ability to write numbers.

Counting the numbers from zero to ten is a valuable preschool activity that a computer program can make into a fascinating game. Helping children recognize number symbols is an added value. Discriminating among the numbers 2 and 3 and 5, for example, calls for finely tuned visual perception and memory. Children learn such discrimination through repetition, an activity that can be provided in every conceivable form by a computer program.

Of course, children need to learn more than recognition. They must comprehend what numbers mean. Again, computer programs serve them well. Computer programs induce children to respond at the level at which they are most comfortable, while challenging them to progress as far as they are able (Beaty 1986, 195-99).

## STICKYBEAR NUMBERS

A second program in the *Stickybear* series presents the numbers 0 through 9 with high-resolution graphics. The graphics are as colorful and interesting to children as those in the alphabet program, but the program works differently. The numbers on the top row of the keyboard control only the number of objects that appear in each scene, not the graphics. There are about a dozen different scenes and about twenty different animated objects that appear randomly when a number is pressed. They are as follows:

| *Scene* | *Object* |
|---|---|
| Blank, colored background | Train, spaceship, or car travels across the scene, apple bounces across diagonally or drum drums with drumstick |
| Blank, colored background with vertical line as a wall | Arrow shoots into the wall |
| Underwater scene | Fish swims nonstop with sound |

| Scene | Object |
|---|---|
| Surface of the moon | Spaceship flies across, star twinkles, or Saturn-shaped planet or satellite flies across |
| Large house with nine windows | Stickybear stands at window and moves his mouth |
| Small house with tree | Airplane or bird flies across the sky |
| Stickybear in a corner | Ball goes over bear's head |
| Mama Stickybear in a corner | Heart flies around the room |
| Stickybear at a table | Stickybear eats ice-cream sundae |
| Ocean and island | Sailboat sails to the tune of "Sailing Sailing" |
| Snow and mountains | Penguin runs around and flaps wings |
| Snow and house | Snowman wears scarf that flaps to a song |

The only written directions, PRESS ANY NUMBER OR USE SPACE BAR, appear in bubble letters after the title. Pressing a number causes a scene with the number symbol in the corner to appear. Next, the corresponding number of objects appears one at a time. The child may then press another number and the cycle repeats with a different scene.

Pressing the space bar after pressing a number generates a different response. The scene remains, but one object is subtracted each time the space bar is pressed. When zero is reached, a new scene appears. If the child starts with the space bar instead of a number, a scene appears followed by objects that increase in number each time the space bar is pressed.

In summary, the child has control over the number of objects, the change of scene, and the addition or subtraction of objects. Children have no control over which objects or scenes appear.

## INTRODUCING THE PROGRAM

In the Elmira Project, *Stickybear Numbers* was introduced to two classes of three and four year olds. All of the children were familiar with the keyboard and had successfully used *Jeepers Creatures* and *Stickybear ABC* programs. The teacher talked to the children as a group about the new program that used numbers instead of letters. She asked them about the numbers that stood for their ages, just as she had asked them about the letters that stood for their names. All of the children knew their ages. Most of the children could count to at least ten.

The teacher then asked the children to find the numbers on the keyboard. None of the children recognized the numbers at first, even though all of them had operated toy cash registers, the typewriter, and the computer keyboard. Finally, someone guessed "the top row." "That's right," the teacher responded. But for the children it was not right, we were soon to discover.

When it was time for free-play activities, none of the children could operate the new program. Although they pressed key after key, none of them touched the number keys. When the teacher asked them where they would find the number keys, no one knew. The teacher finally solved the problem

*At first, young children may have trouble finding the number keys.*

on the first day by putting a template (cut-out paper) over all but the number keys. Of course, the children had no trouble finding the numbers then.

In spite of the teacher's good intentions, this solution did not seem satisfactory in the long run. We were hoping to find that children could use the computer with no templates, gimmicks or crutches. Why couldn't the children find the numbers, we asked ourselves? We had already concluded that if children had to rely on templates, then they were not ready for that particular program. This seemed to be a good rule of thumb for measuring the difficulty of programs (see p. 170).

But, we still did not know why the children had trouble finding number keys. We finally discovered that, unlike letter symbols, number symbols were not familiar to the children. Knowing their ages did not mean they realized that numbers were different from letters. Knowing how to count did not mean they recognized the number symbols.

While most of the three year olds, and all of the fours, could write at least one letter of their name, they had had no experience in writing numbers. There was also great confusion between the graphic symbols for numbers and those for letters. In addition, children still seemed to use a limited number of keys: those in the middle and closest to the bottom of the keyboard. Even after they had learned where the number keys were located, they often made the mistake of pressing I for one, and O for zero. In this particular program, nothing happens when letter keys are pressed.

In an effort to solve our dilemma, we introduced the program to the three year olds in a different way: we showed them an eight-by-ten-inch diagram of the keyboard with the numbers and space bar highlighted. Afterwards, when the teacher asked them to find the numbers on the diagram, all of the children did so without difficulty. When they used the computer, they had no trouble transferring their knowledge to the keyboard and locating the numbers. After that episode we always used our keyboard diagram to introduce a new program that used different keys.

## STAGES IN USING NUMBERS PROGRAM

The stages of manipulation, mastery, and meaning that children experience while learning to use number programs are described below.

### Manipulation

While using the new program, there was at first very little conversation between the partners. One child manipulated the keyboard while the partner watched silently. The two children then alternated, pressing every other key. It was Nick who broke the silence, saying: "I pushed seven arrows."

Most of the children initially tried different numbers, rather than repeating a number. They also tried to change the graphic before the correct number of objects had appeared. It took time for the children to realize that they controlled the number of objects to appear.

Many of the four year olds learned to use the space bar immediately. They enjoyed watching the objects disappear from the screen as each press of the space bar subtracted one. When they reached zero a new scene appeared and new objects began coming into the scene, one by one with every press. Some children abandoned the numbers entirely and used only the space bar.

With the three year olds, the teacher stood by to see if they could find the number keys. She had noted earlier that they quickly left the computer when frustrated. She found that she needed to ask the question, Can anyone find the number keys? Her question helped the children to focus on the task at hand and was a reminder that this game was different.

With the teacher's help, the children did not experience any trouble finding the keys and were soon pressing numbers. The teacher also asked whether they could find the space bar. The children could but most did not use it as readily as the four year olds did.

As with other programs, the children seemed to overgeneralize the rules they had taught themselves. With *Stickybear ABC* each letter controlled two different graphics. Such was not the case with *Stickybear Numbers*. Graphics appeared randomly; thus, the children had no control over them. Consequently, many of the children became frustrated.

Because the children had access to three different game programs, they frequently started *Stickybear Numbers* by pressing letters, too. When they noticed that nothing happened, they switched to numbers exclusively. They did not seem to make any connection between the number they pressed and the number of items that appeared on the screen.

## Mastery

What made the difference in this program was the space bar. Making the objects disappear one by one was exciting to the children. Making the objects reappear one by one was also fun. Once they had solved the riddle of the new program—that number keys controlled only numbers of objects, not the kinds of objects; and that the space bar would add or subtract objects— they were on their way toward learning what the program had to teach.

The use of the space bar to teach counting and one-to-one correspondence was a big plus. We wished that the program had been designed to give the user control over the scenes and kinds of objects. We realized, however, that the computer's memory was a limiting factor. But, we had also observed that the more control the children had, the more they would use a program and, therefore, learn from it.

## Meaning

The games the children invented to make this program meaningful for themselves were different from those for *Stickybear ABC,* because the program itself was different. As the children mastered the program, they became more talkative. Part of their creativity, in fact, was their talk about the graphics. One boy talked about making an airplane when airplanes appeared. It was obvious that the making, or control, was very important to the children.

As the children's expertise grew, they began naming each of the items that appeared, including hearts, flying saucers, and arrows. Arrows were a favorite, and the children kept them on the monitor by pressing the space bar instead of another number. Commented one child, "Would you like to get killed with arrows? They'll kill you."

The children also began counting objects as they appeared on the screen. Johanna, a mature and experienced child, touched one object as it appeared and made no mistakes or skips. It was obvious she had mastered one-to-one correspondence. While her partner pressed the space bar to subtract, she surprised us by saying: "Two take away one makes one. One take away one makes zero."

Most of the children naturally fell into a count-down game. As one child pressed the space bar to subtract, the other counted down: "eight, seven, six, five, four, three, two, one, zero—blast off!" Many of the children touched the objects as they appeared or disappeared from the screen.

Children demonstrated their competitiveness with some of their invented games. For example, one child proclaimed: "I pushed nine. Nine is more than two. There's going to be nine apples. I got more than you!"

The children's comments as they viewed the graphics were fascinating. One child thought that drums looked like flying saucers and houses and that Saturn looked like flying saucers.

Dialogues between partners revealed a high degree of inventiveness. For example, Nick saw the arrows and asked, "Would you like to get killed by one of those?" Kyle, his partner, replied, "No I would run around." When the apples vanished one by one, Nick shouted, "Someone's eating all the apples!" Kyle tried to follow the fish on the screen with his finger. A large fish and several small ones appeared one by one and then disappeared when Nick used the space bar. Said Nick, "Someone is eating the fish." Kyle responded, "The shark ate 'em." If the boys could have called up the same graphic again, a shark game involving numbers and one-to-one correspondence would undoubtedly have ensued. The children then could have played the game repeatedly, gaining more understanding of numbers each time if they had had control over which graphic appeared.

## WHAT CHILDREN LEARNED FROM STICKYBEAR NUMBERS

*Stickybear Numbers* taught the children several things in the course of their exploration of the program.

1. The children learned more about numbers:
   a. That numbers are different from letters
   b. That keyboard numbers are on the top row
   c. That one press of the space bar changes the number of items
   d. That they could count from 0 to 9 and back again by adding or subtracting items with the space bar
   e. That there is a different number name for each item added or subtracted

2. The children induced the rules for the new program

Most children did not notice that the number at the top of the screen also changed every time the space bar added or subtracted items. The children would have learned this if they had been able to control the graphics and, thus, had time to look at ones of their choosing.

Perhaps because there were only ten number symbols, many children went through all ten of them. However, with the letter program, none of the children pressed all twenty-six letters of the alphabet. Letters, of course, are not located all in a row on the keyboard as are numbers.

## ACTIVITIES TO BE USED WITH COMPUTER NUMBER PROGRAMS

Number programs lend themselves to use with counting games, number toys, and counting books, which are described below.

### Counting Games

Your manipulative shelves should be filled with counting games of all sorts. Dice, giant dice, large dominoes, and poker chips can be used by preschoolers in all sorts of ways. Counting, sorting, stacking, building, and manipulating are games young children invent using these counters. A simple board game in which a counter must move across squares helps with counting and one-to-one correspondence. The use of colored cuisenaire rods gives children a large assortment of items to count and sort.

### Number Toys

Rubber number puzzles, wooden puzzle boards, magnetic numbers, peg number boards, counting abacuses, counting blocks, and counting sticks are some of the commercial number toys available. Toy cash registers and play money are especially helpful to use before introducing computer number programs.

## Counting Books

Richard Hefter's *One Bear Two Bears: the Strawberry Number Book* (Middletown, Conn.: Weekly Reader Books, 1980) accompanies the *Stickybear Numbers* program. It shows Stickybears in numbered jogging outfits engaged in a variety of sports while counting rhymes are played.

Robin and Jocelyn Wild's *The Bears' Counting Book* (New York: Harper and Row, 1978) is a funny, turnabout story of three bears (not Stickybears) who go for a walk, find a house where the occupants are gone, and really make a mess of things playing with one clock, two chairs, three beds, all the way through ten. Then they skip to twenty tools, thirty hens, forty cows and fifty apples.

Children will love John Patience's *The Fancy Dress Party Counting Book,* (U.K.: Peter Haddock, n.d.). Each double-spread page shows children in costumes arriving at a birthday party. From two capering clowns to ten royal rulers, the illustrations show marvelous dress-up costumes on contemporary nursery school children. The last pages ask the readers to count candles on the cake, balloons, and glasses of orange juice.

Fulvio Testa's *If You Take a Pencil* (New York: Dial Books for Young Readers, 1982) is a different sort of counting book that invites the reader to start with one pencil, draw two cars, and then proceed through a marvelous series of illustrations that show numbers of things being sequentially added. The story reaches its climax when a buried treasure chest opens to reveal one pencil.

## ONE-TO-ONE CORRESPONDENCE

The concept that a certain number stands for a particular quantity is important for preschoolers to learn. Number games and number symbols will remain abstract concepts to the young child until he or she can match a number with the quantity of concrete objects called for. This matching is the beginning of one-to-one correspondence.

Once children have learned the names and symbols for the numbers 0 to 10, they need to learn what numbers mean. *Stickybear Numbers* included one-to-one correspondence as part of its message to children by having objects appear and disappear one by one.

Children also learn the concept by dealing with concrete objects in their environment. When they set the table for a snack or lunch, they place one cup and one napkin at each place. They put one blanket on each cot for nap time. They give one cupcake to each child at party time. At first, children may have items left over from these activities, just as they did when they pointed to objects and skipped some as they counted. It is difficult for children at this stage in their cognitive development to do one-to-one correspondence tasks with consistency and complete accuracy. What they need is experience and practice with all sorts of matching.

Computer programs can help children explore the various facets of one-to-one correspondence through matching games. Simple matching games have them make pairs by finding an object identical in appearance to another object. More complex matching games have children put objects together on a different basis. Perhaps the objects belong together because they live in a certain dwelling (a horse in a barn, a man in a house, a bird in a nest) or eat a certain food (a horse with hay, a man with a hamburger, a bird with a worm). More complex matching problems ask children to match, for example, the number of birds with the correct number of nests. *Dinosaurs,* a game that employs several matching concepts, is good practice for one-to-one correspondence.


## DINOSAURS

This program contains five matching games about dinosaurs, which appear in order from the simplest to the most complex. Children use the cursor and RETURN keys to operate the program. Pressing ESCAPE takes them back to the menu. The program starts with an illustrated menu and a bouncing ball with which the child chooses one of the games. The simplest game choice is illustrated by six pairs of matched green dinosaurs; the next by one dinosaur eating a plant and another eating a bone; the next by a scene with land, water, and sky; the next by land and water with three rectangles; finally, the most complex game choice is illustrated by the word *Triceratops.* Children choose a game by pressing an arrow key until the bouncing ball comes to rest next to the picture of the desired game. Then they press RETURN and the game appears on the screen.

The menu is a good example of a nonverbal picture menu for preliterate children. Until they try the program, they will not know what each of the game choices is about. However, once children are familiar with the program, the menu provides them with visual clues that will prove more important to them than words.

### Game 1: Matching by Appearance

Five different green dinosaurs appear in a horizontal row at the top of the screen. A green jungle scene with a palm tree and an erupting volcano fills the rest of the screen. A single green dinosaur then lumbers across the screen to the accompaniment of a sound. (Each dinosaur has its own sound.) When the dinosaur stops, the child moves the dinosaur with the arrow keys, making it go back or forward until it is under the correct matching dinosaur. The child then presses the RETURN button and, if a correct match has been made, the pair of dinosaurs flash on and off in a different color, and a tune plays. The first dinosaur then lumbers off and another one appears. If the child makes an incorrect match, nothing happens.

When all six of the dinosaurs have been correctly matched, the child is rewarded by a dinosaur parade of different color dinosaurs moving across the bottom of the screen to music. The parade takes place at the conclusion of each game. Although this reward may seem appealing to an adult, the most rewarding aspect of any program is the child's controlling the actors, not watching them perform on their own.

## Game 2: Matching with Food

In the food-matching game, the top half of the screen is divided vertically, with bones on the right side and plants and flowers on the left. A dinosaur moves across the screen and stops. The child must then match the dinosaur with the food it eats by pressing arrow keys that move the dinosaur up and to the right or to the left. Once a choice has been made, the child presses RETURN. If the choice is correct, the dinosaur gobbles the food and moves to the top of the screen while another beast appears. If the choice is wrong, nothing happens and the child can try again.

The child learns the correct answers in this game through trial and error. Although a coloring book of dinosaurs with a paragraph of information about each animal accompanies the game, three- and four-year-old children cannot be expected to learn abstract concepts, such as that brontosaurus lived on plants, as older children would. What they do learn from this game is that animals can be matched with the food they eat. When the child has correctly placed the six dinosaurs, they again parade across the screen to music.

## Game 3: Matching with Environment

Where do these dinosaurs live: on land, in water, or in the sky? In this game the children move each dinosaur into its proper environment: the land, the water, or into the clouds. If they are correct, the animal does a back-and-forth dance and then stays where it has been placed. If they are incorrect, nothing happens. Again, the children learn the correct answers by trial and error, and the game ends with a dinosaur parade.

## Game 4: Matching Pairs

Three dinosaurs appear, one in each of three rectangles at the top of the screen. Dinosaurs also begin to appear in the jungle scene. When one comes along that is the same as one at the top, the child moves it with an arrow key up toward the matching animal and presses the RETURN key. If the child is wrong, nothing happens. When all three dinosaurs have been paired correctly, another dinosaur parade takes place.

### Game 5: Matching Dinosaurs to Their Names

This game seems inappropriate for preliterate children, but some will figure it out given enough time. A row of green dinosaurs appears at the top of the screen. The name of one of them appears in large, purple letters across the screen below. A bouncing, white ball is controlled by the arrow keys. The child moves the ball to the dinosaur being named and presses RETURN. If the child has matched the dinosaur and name correctly, the animal lights up and positions itself next to its name. If the child is incorrect, nothing happens. Again, the parade takes place at the end. Children should learn from this game that names of animals can be represented by words and that each of the dinosaurs has a different name.

## ACTIVITIES TO BE USED WITH DINOSAURS

Children are intrigued by dinosaurs and other such "monsters." Preliterate children can be motivated by games like these to strengthen their understanding of one-to-one correspondence. However, teachers who include a dinosaur program in their software library must remember to integrate it into the curriculum.

Miniature plastic dinosaurs can be purchased through school supply companies and placed in the block corner with the zoo and farm animals. This particular computer program may also interest children in trying to move as dinosaurs do. Try some creative movement activities to the rhythm of drum beats or clapping. There are many dinosaur books that can be read aloud or kept in your book area. *Bruno Brontosaurus* by Nicole Rubel (New York: Avon Books, 1983) tells a funny tale of a baby brontosaurus born into a family of tyrannosaurs. Bruno has a great deal of trouble eating because of his taste for plants, while his family likes only meat.

## OBSERVING CHILDREN USING NUMBERS AND MATCHING COMPUTER PROGRAMS

When children are playing with the numbers and matching programs, sit or stand close enough to hear what they are saying as you observe and record. Place a tape recorder on the table next to the computer, if you have one. Children pay no attention to it, and you will be able to record everything that is said. Be sure to transcribe it soon afterwards so that the words are meaningful to you. The children's dialogues will add a great deal to your understanding of their development in the area of cognition. What should you listen for?

Can the child count without skipping any numbers? Does he or she count both forward and backward? Does the child match numbers with objects (one-to-one correspondence)? What does the child say about matching? How do children teach their partners what to do?

The answer to the last question is crucial. If a child truly understands a concept, the best indication is the ability to teach it to another child. The child may only be teaching the operation of the program, but listen carefully because he or she may very well mention something about numbers.

## REFERENCES

**Beaty, Janice J.** *Observing Development of the Young Child.* Columbus, Ohio: Merrill Publishing Co., 1986.

**Billings, Karen.** "Developing Mathematical Concepts with Microcomputer Activities." *The Arithmetic Teacher,* (February 1983): 19-62.

**Cowan, Philip A.** *Piaget with Feeling.* New York: Holt, Rinehart and Winston, 1978.

**Ferrerio, Emilia,** and **Ana Teberosky.** *Literacy before Schooling* (translated from Spanish). Exeter, N.H.: Heinemann Educational Books, 1979.

**Osborn, Janie Dyson,** and **D. Keith Osborn.** *Cognition in Early Childhood.* Athens, Ga.: Education Associates, 1983.

**Richardson, Lloyd I., et al.** *A Mathematics Activity Curriculum for Early Childhood and Special Education.* New York: Macmillan Co., 1980.

**Spitzer, Dean, J.** *Concept Formation and Learning in Early Childhood.* Columbus, Ohio: Merrill Publishing Co., 1977.

## SOFTWARE

*Charlie Brown's 123s*
      Random House
      201 E. 50th St.
      New York, N.Y. 10022
Apple II family; high-resolution graphics
A cleverly done program in which children press a number and that number of

"Peanuts" characters appear; or the program asks for a number, and if correctly given, a long, animated "Snoopy" graphic appears.

### Dinosaurs

> Advanced Ideas, Inc.
> 2550 Ninth St., Suite 104
> Berkeley, Calif. 94710

Apple II family; IBM, Acorn; Commodore 64
Discussed in this chapter. (Grades preschool–3)

### Finger Abacus

> Edutek Corp.
> P.O. Box 2560
> Palo Alto, Calif. 94702

Apple II with Applesoft ROM; 32 K
Counting numbers 0 to 99 on a finger abacus with practice in number representation through a discovery- and game-oriented program. Somewhat advanced for preschoolers. (Grades preschool-Kindergarten through 6)

### Learning with Leeper

> Sierra On-Line, Inc.
> P.O. Box 485
> Coarsegold, Calif. 93614

Apple II family
Two of the games on this program teach children matching and counting skills with various pictures, including dogs and bones. Discussed in chapter 8. (Grades preschool-1)

### Match-up!

> Hayden Software Co.
> 600 Suffolk St.
> Lowell, Mass. 01853

Atari, 400, 800, Atari tape 16K, Atari disk 24K; Commodore 64; memory required
In this matching program children put objects into appropriate groups, pick out objects that don't belong, and learn to pair objects. (Grades preschool-1)

### Micro Habitats

> Reader's Digest Software
> Microcomputer Software Division
> Pleasantville, N.Y. 10570

Apple II family; Commodore 64; IBM PC, PCjr; 48K
This program has some similarity to *Dinosaurs*. Three environments are used: an underwater garden, outer space, and the jungle. Children must decide what kind of animal and plant life should be matched with the proper habitat. (Grades preschool-3)

### Mindplay: Cat 'n Mouse

> Methods and Solutions
> 300 Unicorn Park Drive
> Woburn, Mass. 01801

Apple II family; high-resolution graphics
The program has mazes at different levels, is like *Learning with Leepers,* and uses arrow keys instead of a joystick.

### *Musical Mathematics*

> Hayden Software
> 600 Sufflok St.
> Lowell, Mass. 01853

Apple II family, 48K
This is a high-resolution, animated, sound/graphics program that introduces children to the basics of math through music.

### *Number Farm*

> Developmental Learning Materials
> 1 DLM Park, P.O. Box 5000
> Allen, Tex. 75002

Children learn number and counting skills from six games, each based on a farm theme. (Grades preschool-2)

### *Stickybear Numbers*

> Weekly Reader Family Software
> A Division of Xerox Education Publications
> Middletown, Conn. 06457

Apple II family, 48K; Atari, 48K; Commodore 64
Discussed in this chapter. (Grades preschool–1)

## LEARNING ACTIVITIES

1. Have a child who knows how teach you how to use a numbers program. What did you learn from this? What do you think the child has learned from the program? How can you tell?

2. Read a counting book to a child or small group of children after they have used a similar computer program. What do they have to say about the concepts in the book? What do you think they have learned from the computer program?

3. Make up a matching or lotto game and play it with a child after he or she has used the computer program. What has he or she learned about the concept involved?

4. Observe and record a child as he or she uses the numbers program. What does he or she seem to know about numbers? How can you tell?

5. Ask a child who knows a matching program to teach another child how to use it. Observe and record the results. What did you learn about the two children and their knowledge of the concepts involved?

# The Computer as a Building Block

P laying with blocks is an activity most children have engaged in before they enter preschool. Alphabet blocks, stacking blocks, snap blocks, unit blocks, hollow blocks, plastic blocks, foam rubber blocks, and Lego bricks are some of the kinds of blocks with which children may have experience. Both parents and teachers encourage this activity because children seem to enjoy it. Youngsters exhibit their developing creativity and small motor skills when balancing blocks on top of one another to build representational buildings. Child development specialists, however, have learned that children are really doing more.

Block building is one of those early childhood activities with hidden benefits for children because it involves them with a three-dimensional medium that they must act upon not only physically, but cognitively. Playing with blocks allows them to convert abstract concepts into concrete forms they can begin to understand. Blocks are truly toys for thinking.

Children are forced to consider size and shape as they choose which blocks to use. As they build, they must think about length, width, height, and balance. They need to decide: Which one will fit best? How can I get my truck through the tunnel? Why won't my car go into this garage? What do I have to do to get this bridge over the river? How big should I make this house so the doll's bed will fit?''

While struggling to resolve their block-building problems, young children eventually extract meaning from abstract concepts and apply it. Thus, blocks are marvelous tools for converting thoughts to reality, for making ideas meaningful, and especially for learning to test which possibilities work best.

According to Swiss psychologist Jean Piaget, logical thought is based on the concepts of number, space, and time (Piaget and Inhelder 1967). When children play with blocks, they deal with spatial relationships concretely and meaningfully. For their cognitive development to progress, young children need opportunities, such as block building, to explore, experiment, and make discoveries on their own about spatial relationships.

There are three different aspects of spatial relationships that children need to learn: proximity (near versus far), separation (where one object ends and another begins), and enclosure (open versus closed and inside versus outside) (Richardson 1980). Children acquire knowledge of spatial relationships by interacting with objects, such as blocks, in their environment.

The ability to distinguish between near and far objects (proximity) begins at birth when babies first reach for things. Later, the concept becomes more complex as the toddler starts exploring the environment. Near becomes something more than the objects that can be touched by reaching. Far depends on where in the environment one happens to be.

When children develop separation, they are able to perceive whether objects that touch are a part of one another. Babies learn that they are separate human beings, not a part of mother. Through exploration, the toddler finds out that the chain is part of the light fixture, but that the toy train engine can be separated.

The third aspect of spatial relationships concerns "enclosure," the ability to discriminate between something inside and something outside or whether a figure is open or closed. Children who have not fully developed this cognitive ability often confuse the letters C and O.

Many activities in the preschool classroom help children convert these abstract concepts into a meaningful part of their cognitive development, whether teachers are aware of it or not. Teachers can become aware of how their children are doing with respect to spatial relationships, however, by providing them with computer programs involving such concepts. Although computer programs can never replace concrete experiences, they can add another dimension to learning.

## THE COMPUTER AS A BUILDING BLOCK

A computer program that involves opposites in location or size is a good place to begin. Other programs to consider involve the basic shapes of objects. Some programs that feature building things from shapes or parts are too complex for preschoolers, but other building-type programs will be considered in chapter 9, "The Computer as a Chatterbox."

Your children already know a great deal about opposites. Ask most preschoolers, What is the opposite of short? And they will answer, Tall. Understanding this concept involves experience with real objects in the environment and development of the terminology used to express opposites. Computer programs can help children learn and practice these ideas.

## STICKYBEAR OPPOSITES

We introduced the third program in the *Stickybear* series to the two classes of three year olds and four year olds during the fourth week of the Elmira Project. After the title appeared, the screen displayed: "Choose K for keyboard or P for Paddle." Because we preferred that the children learn to use the keyboard if at all possible, we instructed them to press K. Although they could not read the display, the letter K cued them on what to do next.

This particular game is played by pressing the two arrow keys to animate the character or object in the graphic and by pressing the space bar to change graphics. Twenty-five high-resolution sound/graphics appear randomly to illustrate examples of opposites. The right arrow key controls one extreme of the opposite and its corresponding word, and the left arrow key controls the other. For example:

| *Scene* | *Word* |
|---|---|
| Stickybear walking up stairs | UP |
| Stickybear walking down stairs | DOWN |
| Stickybear walking up a hill | UP |
| Stickybear walking down a hill | DOWN |
| Stickybear climbing up a ladder | TOP |
| Stickybear climbing down a ladder | BOTTOM |
| Low ball bouncing | LOW |
| High ball bouncing | HIGH |
| Stickybear on low side of seesaw | LOW |
| Stickybear on high side of seesaw | HIGH |
| Stickybear in front of fence | IN FRONT |
| Stickbear behind fence | BEHIND |
| Ball bouncing in front of wall | IN FRONT |
| Ball bouncing behind wall | BEHIND |
| Bird zooming across sky | FAST |
| Bird flying slowly across sky | SLOW |
| Pump with parts working rapidly | FAST |
| Pump with parts working slowly | SLOW |
| Road with car zooming toward viewer | NEAR |
| Road with car backing away | FAR |
| Glass filling up | FULL |
| Glass emptying | EMPTY |

| Scene | Word |
|---|---|
| Eight bouncing balls | MANY |
| Three bouncing balls | FEW |
| Stickybear with eyes and mouth open | OPEN |
| Stickybear with eyes and mouth closed | CLOSED |
| Stickybear with smiling mouth and eyes | HAPPY |
| Stickybear with downcast mouth and eyes | SAD |
| Airplane flying over bridge | OVER |
| Airplane flying under bridge | UNDER |
| Green stoplight | GO |
| Red stoplight | STOP |
| Stickybear jumping onto box | ON |
| Stickybear jumping off of box | OFF |
| Stickybear jumping into box | IN |
| Stickybear jumping out of box | OUT |
| Stickybear waving from window of house | INSIDE |
| Mama Stickybear coming out of house | OUTSIDE |
| Door opening | OPEN |
| Door closed | CLOSED |
| Mama Stickybear with hand on lighted lamp | LIGHT |
| Room blackened, except for white eyes | DARK |
| Day scene | DAY |
| Night scene | NIGHT |
| Stickybear with back to viewer | BACK |
| Stickybear facing front | FRONT |
| Car moving across screen | FORWARD |
| Car moving backward across screen | BACKWARD |
| Plant growing to top of screen | TALL |
| Plant shrinking back into pot | SHORT |

## INTRODUCING THE PROGRAM

The teacher introduced the concept of opposites at circle time during the fourth week of the study. The children talked about opposites, named some, and played a circle game using opposites. Then, the teacher read a book about opposites. Although she had cut up the *Stickybear Opposites* poster that accompanied the program into a board game about opposites, it seemed to confuse the children until they had mastered the computer game. After the children had finished the preliminary activities, the teacher showed them the keyboard diagram and had them locate the two arrow keys they would be using.

## STAGES IN USING THE OPPOSITES PROGRAM

Children progressed rapidly with *Stickybear Opposites*. They moved through the three learning stages with no difficulty, as we shall discuss below.

### Manipulation

The four year olds caught on to the game right away. They understood that the right arrow key controlled one part of the animation and the left arrow key controlled the opposite part. Because each child worked the keyboard with a partner, taking turns came naturally. One child pressed the right key, and the other pressed the left key. The only exception in either class was a three-year-old girl who used two fingers at once to manipulate both keys. The other children had great fun with partners, alternating every press of the arrow key. The four year olds giggled and laughed aloud a great deal.

Several of the children tried pressing letter and number keys to see what would happen. When nothing did, they went back to pressing the arrow keys. As with their initial contact with other programs, the children talked little at first. One experienced partner would show the other new partner how the program worked, and away they would go, pressing keys and watching.

### Mastery

Children mastered this program more quickly than any of the other programs. Not only was it simple to operate, but it lent itself well to use by partners. Furthermore, it gave partners more control over the animation for a single graphic than had any of the other programs. The children favored graphics with more exaggerated movement. They played with one up-down graphic for five minutes at a time without changing to a new one.

### Meaning

The children attributed their own meaning to this program not so much by creating new games as by inventing solutions to problems. When they found that they could not control which of the twenty-five graphics would appear, they found a creative solution: they pressed the space bar to change the graphic if it was one that they did not understand or were not attracted to.

*Computer programs can be introduced through storybooks.*

Thus, they went rather quickly through the uninteresting graphics, until they came to a favorite. When they found a particularly appealing graphic, they stayed with it for an exceptionally long period of time. Exaggerated movement and sound seemed the key attractions.

The seesaw was the most popular with all of the children. They pushed the two arrow keys repeatedly, never seeming to tire of watching the seesaw move. Making Stickybear turn around in the back-front graphic was another favorite. They also enjoyed watching the plant grow and then shrink back into the pot in the tall-short graphic and making Stickybear go up and down the stairs and ladder in the up-down and top-bottom graphics.

The children skipped over graphics they did not understand, such as the fast-slow pump, the many-few balls, and the in front of-behind balls. The airplane going over and under the bridge had no sound; they skipped that too.

Inventing games other than pushing the two arrow keys did not seem to be the point here; however, it is certainly possible that with more time several invented games would have emerged. One pair of boys did create their own key-pressing pattern. Each raised his hand high, lowered it to touch the arrow key, and then retracted his hand very quickly. Another boy made up stories. For the top-botton ladder graphic he imagined Stickybear a robber.

## WHAT CHILDREN LEARNED FROM STICKYBEAR OPPOSITES

*Stickybear Opposites* taught the children several things. Some of those are described below:

1. A new turn-taking method

2. The use of the opposite arrow keys

3. Reinforcement for the meaning of opposites

4. The rules for the new program

## BOOKS TO READ ABOUT OPPOSITES

The children seemed to gain more insight into opposites when books featuring opposites were read to them, both before the computer program was introduced and while it was being used.

Stan and Jan Berenstain's *Inside Outside Upside Down* (New York: Random House, 1968) features the Berenstain bears in a funny adventure with a box and a truck. Up-down, off-on, in-out, and inside-outside are the opposites that play a role in this story.

P.D. Eastman's *Big Dog. . .Little Dog: A Bedtime Story* (New York: Random House, 1973) takes big dog Fred and little dog Ted to a ski resort where they are given beds that don't fit. Big-little, fast-slow, upstairs-downstairs, and uphill-downhill are among the opposites used.

Richard Hefter's *Yes and No: A Book of Opposites* (Weekly Reader Books, 1975) accompanies the computer program. Happy-sad, smile-frown, yes-no, full-empty, plain-fancy, light-heavy, pull-push, straight-crooked, high-low, up-down, hill-valley, and smooth-rough are a few of the many opposites featured on every page. This is not a storybook but shows the Stickybears and others illustrating the concepts.

Eric Hill's *More Opposites, Peek-A-Book* (Los Angeles: Price/Stern/Sloan, 1984) is a favorite of preschoolers because they can do something with it other than sit and listen. On each double-page spread there is the question, What is the opposite of. . .? and a large picture, part of which can be lifted for the answer. The opposite of hairy, for instance, can be discovered by lifting up a man's hat to see that his head is bald. Inside the hat is the word *bald*.

Pat Hutchins's *Titch* (New York: Penguin Books, 1971) is another favorite about the little boy Titch, who is unable to do the things that his big brother and sister do until a seed he plants grows into a giant plant. The story should remind listeners of the plant in their computer program.

Catherine Petrie's *Joshua James Likes Trucks* (Chicago: Children's Press, 1982) is a small format book about a little boy who loves trucks of all sizes and shapes.

Giles Reed's *Learn Opposites with the Munch Bunch* (Chicago: Rand McNally and Co., 1981) shows personified vegetables, such as Zach Zucchini and Supercool Cucumber, involved in a host of opposite actions.

## OBSERVING CHILDREN USING OPPOSITES PROGRAMS

Listen to or record what the children are saying about the program. Partners frequently talk to one another, telling each other what to do or what is happening on the screen. Sometimes they ask questions. Statements and questions give the adult observer clues to the children's thinking process. You may find that certain children are reading some of the simple words. On the other hand, if you hear a child say up-down for Stickybear on the ladder, you will know that he or she is not reading the words of the graphic, which are top-bottom.

Another important observation concerns the children's favorite graphics. It is always important for teachers to know what really interests children. You will be able to tell which graphics are most popular by watching which ones children return to most often and by keeping track of how long they spend on various scenes. If you note that the children concentrate on the *Stickybear* up-down graphic with the seesaw, you may want to bring into your classroom a small indoor seesaw. In addition to large-motor skills, your children can physically demonstrate the up-down, high-low, and top-bottom concepts.

Children need experience with concrete objects to assimilate new ideas. The more interested they are with something, the more relevant it becomes to them. You can learn what your children's particular interests are by carefully observing them as they use computer programs.

## SHAPES

Children need to distinguish among the various basic shapes. The human brain seems to be programmed to absorb information about things and to categorize it according to the basic patterns. The "enclosed" basic shapes include the circle, square, rectangle, and triangle. The oval and diamond may also be considered at the preschool level.

Although visual perception plays an important role in determining shapes, the initial identification of shapes by young children involves more than this. What they see is not what they initially get. It is hard for adults to understand that children at first have difficulty differentiating one shape from another. Why can't they see that a circle is different from a square?

The problem seems to involve the Piagetian concept of enclosure. Until children become aware of a shape's features, they categorize circles and squares as the same because both have closed boundaries (Richardson 1980). In other words, their brains overgeneralize about shapes, just as they do about adding *ed* to all verbs to make them past tense. Children need concrete experiences with the roundness of circles and the corners of squares before they can distinguish one from another.

Studies have shown that shape perception is one of the first to appear in young children, even before color perception. Preschoolers, however, often confuse the two, just as they do numbers and letters. Ask a three year old the shape of an object, and the child may very well tell you its color (Richardson 1980). This confusion should prompt preschool teachers to make sure their shape activities feature only shape at first, not color.

Many commercial products come with multi-colored shapes, and although they are attractive to the adult purchaser, they confuse the young child. If children are to learn shapes, then they must be provided with shapes of the same color and material.

Once children understand the concept of circle, then they should begin to identify similar shapes in their environment that look like a circle. Take the children on a "circle walk." What might they find? How about wheels, tires, casters on furniture, clocks, a fishbowl, a doorknob? Once children understand roundness, introduce a new shape: the square. Children need to have enough time to absorb one concept before moving on to a different one.

## STICKYBEAR SHAPES

Computer programs that feature shapes should be used as a follow-up to concrete shape experiences and activities in the classroom. Not only do such programs reinforce the shape concepts already acquired by the children, but they also tell the teacher just where each individual stands regarding his knowledge of shapes.

*Stickybear Shapes* was the most complex program used thus far in the Elmira Project. After the title appeared, the screen asked the children to choose K for keyboard, P for paddle, or M for mouse. We asked our children to press K for keyboard because we wanted them to use the computer keyboard as they had been doing. We felt that a paddle or a mouse was one step removed from the keyboard and, thus, more abstract. In addition, we knew from experience that a paddle or mouse tended to be a one-person implement that caused turn-taking problems.

Once the children had pressed K for keyboard, a word menu appeared asking them to:

*CHOOSE*

1. PICK IT

2. NAME IT

3. FIND IT

Our children did not, of course, read the choices, so we instructed them to choose game one by pressing the space bar when the number 1 was flashing. To choose any of the games, the computer operator could use the cursor until the corresponding number was flashing and then press the space bar.

## Game One: "Pick It"

"Pick It" consists of ten scenes that appear in a consistent order, one after the other. Each scene has one missing piece of a certain shape. Children have to determine what shape is missing and then pick it from the row of shapes at the bottom of the screen. To choose, the operator presses either arrow key, thus making each of the shapes light up in turn. There are five shapes: circle, square, triangle, rectangle, and diamond. When the desired shape is flashing, the operator presses the space bar to choose it. If the child is correct, the missing part of the scene is filled in and the graphic becomes animated. If the child is incorrect, a blatting, raspberry sound is made. Then the child can try again.

SCENE 1: Living room scene with TV set
Missing: Square of TV set
Animation: Stickybear appears on TV and dances to tune

SCENE 2: Flower with butterfly on it
Missing: Diamond body of butterfly
Animation: Body appears and wings of butterfly open and close

SCENE 3: Stickybear in car
Missing: Wheels on car
Animation: Wheels appear and car appears to move across screen

SCENE 4: Hand with ring
Missing: Diamond from ring
Animation: Diamond appears on ring and sparkles

SCENE 5: Stickybear pushing boy in wagon
Missing: Rectangular body of wagon
Animation: Body of wagon appears and wheels rotate to tune

SCENE 6: Stickybear in bed with alarm clock on stand
Missing: Circular face of clock
Animation: Clock face appears and clock rings loudly

SCENE 7: Box with ball next to it
Missing: Square face of box
Animation: Box face appears, top opens, and jack-in-the-box pops out to
    a tune

SCENE 8: Boy Stickybear next to cake with candles
Missing: Rectangular body of cake
Animation: Whole cake appears and boy blows out candles

SCENE 9: Seashore and sailboat
Missing: Triangular sail of sailboat
Animation: Sail appears, boat bobs on water, crab scuttles on shore

SCENE 10: Moonscape with spaceship
Missing: Nose cone of spaceship
Animation: Nose cone appears and robot bounces

## Game Two: "Name It"

This particular game is for literate children. A word in lowercase letters
appears on the screen: circle, square, rectangle, triangle, or diamond. At the
bottom of the screen are the five shapes in blue. Pressing an arrow key makes
one of the shapes flash. The child must choose the correct flashing shape
and press the space bar. If the child is correct, an outline of the shape appears
and bounces around the word; if incorrect, a raspberry sound is heard.

## Game Three: "Find It"

This game is similar to "Pick It." There are eight scenes that appear one
at a time on the screen. A shape name and outline appear randomly at the
bottom of each scene. Each press of an arrow key lights up a shape some-
where in the scene. When the shape lights up that matches the shape at
the bottom of the screen, the child is to press the space bar. If the child is
correct, the scene becomes animated; if incorrect, a raspberry sound is heard.

Even though words are used, this game seems easier than "Pick It" because only one shape, instead of five, appears at the bottom of the screen.

SCENE 1: Stickybear sitting on couch
Key controls: triangular pillow, circular lamp base, diamond couch design, square end table, rectangular couch leg
Animation: Stickybear swings leg to tune

SCENE 2: Street scene at corner with Stickybear in car
Key controls: square, triangular, rectangular, and diamond street signs; circular rearview mirror on car
Animation: Stickybear turns steering wheel and horn toots

SCENE 3: Stickybear putting star on Christmas tree
Key controls: diamond present, square present, rectangular stool, circular ornament, triangular ornament
Animation: Christmas tree lights up and snow falls outside window

SCENE 4: Toy box and toys
Key controls: diamond on drum, circular cushion, square chimney on toy house, triangular block, rectangular toy box
Animation: Drum beats to tune and toy bear waves

SCENE 5: Steam locomotive on track
Key controls: rectangular engine, diamond smokestack, circular wheel, square cab, triangular cowcatcher
Animation: Train moves to sound and Stickybear waves from cab

SCENE 6: Seashore with Boy Stickybear and kite
Key controls: diamond kite, circular sun, triangular sail on sailboat, square house, rectangular door
Animation: Kite flutters, water moves, flag on boat waves

SCENE 7: Kitchen with Mama Stickybear
Key controls: diamond design on wallpaper, circle design on stove, square pot, triangular pot cover, rectangular frying pan
Animation: pot bubbles, Mama stirs something in bowl

SCENE 8: Stickybear in basket of hot-air balloon
Key controls: diamond design on balloon, circular sun, square balloon basket, triangular design on balloon, rectangular top of basket
Animation: Stickybear throws balls out of basket

## INTRODUCING THE PROGRAM

*Stickybear Shapes* should not be used with children who are unfamiliar with the concept of shapes. Preschoolers should have several concrete experiences in identifying shapes before attempting a computer program at this level. The complexity of the program also means that prior computer experience is important for preschool children to succeed using the self-discovery method. "Pick It," for instance, involves a five-step process: (1) children must recognize what is missing from the scene; (2) they must decide the shape of the missing part; (3) they must find the correct shape at the bottom of the screen; (4) they must press the arrow key until that shape lights up; and (5) they must press the space bar to make their choice.

We introduced the program after the two classes of children were familiar with *Jeepers Creatures*, *Stickybear ABC*, *Stickybear Numbers*, and *Stickybear Opposites* (see table 6, p. 175). The teacher brought shape pillows on the morning the new program was to be introduced. The children had no trouble identifying circle, square, triangle, and rectangle. The diamond was a somewhat unfamiliar shape. The *Stickybear* poster that accompanies the program had been mounted on cardboard and was used in a matching game with the children. Circles, squares, triangles, rectangles, and diamonds had been cut out of cardboard, and the children had to match the cutouts to similar shapes in the poster illustration.

Once again, teacher and children discussed how to use the arrow keys. The teacher pointed out that the keys would be used somewhat differently than they had been in *Stickybear Opposites*.

## STAGES IN USING STICKYBEAR SHAPES

Due to some of the complexities of *Stickybear Shapes*, children progressed more slowly through the learning stages. Nonetheless, they were totally absorbed by its graphics and sound.

### Manipulation

At first, the children enjoyed looking at the scene that appeared, but it took a while before they associated the blinking shapes at the bottom of the screen with pressing the arrow keys. The operator could press either of the two arrow keys and make each shape light up in turn. Children had trouble understanding that when they pressed the right arrow key, the blinking light would move to the right and when they pressed the left arrow key, it would move left.

Children also found it difficult to choose the correct blinking shape with the space bar because they often overshot their mark. Such difficulty may have been due to the lag between pressing the key and movement of the blinking light to the next shape. However, once they got the idea to press the space bar when the correct shape lighted up, they loved the game. Many children made their selection by trial and error but, nevertheless, learned the rather complex concept involved: that they had to decide what shape was missing and then select a similar shape from those at the bottom. Some of the shapes were difficult for an adult to choose, not to mention a four year old. But, almost anyone can learn the correct shapes through trial and error.

## Mastery

Once children learned the correct shapes, they continued to play sometimes for as long as forty-five minutes. Partners took turns either watching or playing. They became totally engrossed in the graphics. Children spent a great deal of time on one graphic before making the correct choice and being able to move on to the next one.

The reinforcer in this program was animation of the graphic, which in fact was quite elaborate. Adults who played the program for the first time tried to guess what would be animated in the scenes. The scene that was hardest to second-guess was Stickybear in the hot-air balloon. No one could have guessed Stickybear throwing balls. When Stickybear appeared on the TV and danced to music, one child looked up and asked, "Does that mean I won the game?"

Although the negative reinforcer sounded like a raspberry, it was not very loud and did not seem to bother the children. We would have preferred that the program not respond with a negative reinforcer such as sound. In some instances, children chose a wrong answer just to hear the strange noise! Additionally, the negative sound was often embarrassing to the child who made the mistake because it called everyone's attention to the error. We believe it is better for programs to do nothing when an incorrect choice is made.

## Meaning

Because we introduced the program near the end of our study, none of the children progressed to the point of creating their own meanings from the program. Most of the children were still at the mastery stage in which they had induced the rules but still had to struggle to find the correct shape. Some of the youngsters were still manipulating the arrow keys and trying with only moderate success to stop at the desired shape. None of the children was able to go through the entire program at one sitting.

## WHAT CHILDREN LEARNED FROM STICKYBEAR SHAPES

In spite of its more complex format, children learned several things from *Stickybear Shapes*. Those are

1. Refinement of their concepts of circle, square, triangle, rectangle, and diamond

2. Refinement of their visual perception while searching for and finding missing shapes in a complex scene

3. Practice in identifying parts and wholes

4. The rules for a new program

5. Manipulation of the arrow keys

6. A longer attention span

## BOOKS TO READ ABOUT SHAPES AND BUILDING

In addition to block building and other classroom activities involving shapes, there are a number of concept books about shapes that will help children to reinforce the ideas they learn through computer shape programs.

Byron Barton's *Building a House* (New York: Puffin Books, 1981) is a simple, colorful book that shows step-by-step, from the hole dug by the bulldozer to the family moving in, how a house is built. Simple text on one page is illustrated by a full-color drawing on the adjacent page. Builders, bricklayers, carpenters, plumbers, electricians, and painters are shown working.

Richard Hefter's *The Strawberry Book of Shapes* (Weekly Reader Books, 1976), which accompanies the computer program, shows the Stickybears and their friends in nonsensical shapes and positions with a rhyming line of text on every other page.

Bill Gillham and Susan Hulme's *Let's Look for Shapes* (New York: Coward-McCann, 1984) is a small format book containing colored photographs of shapes in the children's environment on one page and a child using a similarly shaped object on the facing page.

Pat Hutchins's *Changes, Changes* (New York: Puffin Books, 1971) is a wordless picture book showing a wooden man and wooden woman who use the same set of wooden blocks over and over to build the necessary objects to get them out of their predicaments. The objects include a house, fire truck, boat, and train.

## OBSERVING CHILDREN USING SHAPE PROGRAMS

First of all, children need to be able to find the shapes. As you observe, you may notice children pointing to the shapes or touching the screen. Next you will want to know if they can name the shapes. Are they familiar with the triangle? What about the diamond? What do they say about the shapes? Do they make comparisons with other things in the scene or with objects in the room? For preschoolers it is not necessary that they recognize the words for each of the shapes.

In addition to the concepts they are learning, you will want to observe how children manipulate the keys. Can they control the arrow keys and space bar in order to choose the correct shape? Do they choose by guessing? By trial and error? By knowing the correct shape, moving the cursor, and pressing the space bar? The last action will tell you that the child is a sophisticated player who has induced the rules for the program and is able to manipulate the keys to carry them out.

What about the children's attention span on this program? Those who really understand the program usually want to play it for long periods of time. Those who don't seldom stay with it for long. Children who choose shapes haphazardly have little control over the animation because they do not understand what makes it move. Because control is a big issue with preschoolers, they often leave a program in frustration if they find they lack control. Thus, it is important to note how long players stay with a game and how many of its scenes they finish.

Do any of the children invent their own games for this program? If they have played with it long enough, they should progress to the meaning stage and impart their own meaning by making up something new to do with the program.

# REFERENCES

Beaty, Janice J. *Observing Development of the Young Child.* Columbus, Ohio: Merrill Publishing Co., 1986.

Beaty, Janice J., and W. Hugh Tucker. *Computer in the Preschool: An Integrated Activity.* 1985. Elmira, N.Y.: 3-to-5, P.O. Box 3213, 14905. Slides and Tape.

Hirsch, Elisabeth S., ed. *The Block Book.* Washington, D.C.: National Association for the Education of Young Children, 1984.

Piaget, Jean. *Play, Dreams and Imitation in Childhood.* New York: Norton, 1962.

Piaget, Jean, and B. Inhelder. *The Child's Conception of Space.* New York: Norton, 1967.

Reifel, Stuart. "Block Construction: Children's Developmental Landmarks in Representation of Space." *Young Children,* November 1984: 61–67.

Richardson, Lloyd I., Kathy L. Goodman, Nancy Noftsinger Hartman, and
Henri C. LePique. *A Mathematics Activity Curriculum for Early
Childhood and Special Education.* New York: Macmillan Co., 1980.

Swigger, Kathlen, and James Campbell. "The Computer Goes to Nursery
School." *Educational Computer,* (July–August 1981): 10–12.

Watt, Molly. "Electronic Thinker Toys." *Popular Computing,* (June 1983):
161–72.

# SOFTWARE

### *Juggle's Rainbow*

The Learning Company
545 Middlefield Rd.
Menlo Park, Calif. 94025

Apple II family, 48K, disk drive, DOS 3.3; Atari 400, 800, 48K, disk drive, DOS;
Commodore 64; 1982

Already a classic, this first-generation learning program that involves children
with the concepts of above-below and left-right while building a stylized rainbow, a butterfly, or a windmill is one of the early colorful learning games for
children. A blue bar comes with the program to divide the keyboard for the
youngest users. Most preschoolers do not really need such help. In addition, a
new generation of preschool computer programs with complex illustrations has
lured children away from programs like this with its simple graphics. (Grades
preschool–1)

### *Shape and Color Rodeo*

Developmental Learning Materials
One DLM Park, P.O. Box 5000
Allen, Tex. 75002

Apple II family, DOS 3.3, disk drive

Six sequenced games involve children with the concepts of shape and color:
"Shape Roundup," a hidden-shape game; "Cowhand Brand," a shape-matching
game with brands; "Color Mix-and-Match," a color-blending and matching
game; "Rope Trick," a shape-sequence game; "Color Mix-and-Match 2" for two
players; and "Rodeo Flags," a pick-which-one-is-different game. (Grades
preschool–2)

### *Shape-up!*

Hayden Software Co.
600 Suffolk St.
Lowell, Mass. 01853

Atari 400, 800, tape 16K, disk 24K; Commodore 64, memory required

This is a program to teach young children shape recognition. (Grades preschool–1)

*Stickers*

> Springboard Software, Inc.
> 7807 Creekridge Circle
> Minneapolis, Minn. 55435

Apple II family; IBM PC and PCjr; Commodore 64; 1984

This program presents an interesting concept of building pictures with various shapes called stickers that are shown at the bottom of each screen. Ten different figures from animals and monsters to spaceships and vehicles can be constructed with the stickers by directing a cursor to pick up the sticker and move it to the space on the figure. Either a joystick or the I, J, K, and M keys control the movements. Stickers can be painted different colors, rotated to fit the figure, cut out, and saved and printed out. The program, however, is very complicated for preschoolers because there are so many steps, and because it takes so long to fill in one figure with the proper stickers. Older children or younger children with home computers will have more success. (Grades K–6)

*Stickybear Opposites*

> Weekly Reader Family Software
> A Division of Xerox Education Publications
> Middletown, Conn. 06457

Apple II family, DOS 3.3, 48K; disk drive
Discussed in this chapter. (Grades K–1)

*Stickybear Shapes*

> Weekly Reader Family Software
> A Division of Xerox Education Publications
> Middletown, Conn. 06457

Apple II family, DOS 3.3
Discussed in this chapter. (Grades K–1)

*Tonk in the Land of Buddy-Bots*

> Mindscape, Inc.
> 3444 Dundee Rd.
> Northbrook, Ill. 60062

Apple II family 64K; Atari; Commodore 64; IBM PC with graphics, color
> adapter, and enhanced; IBM PCjr, memory required

In this program of shapes and patterns, children collect the different body parts of a Buddy-Bot and put him together. (Grades preschool–3)

*Train Set*

> Harper and Row
> Orders to: Keystone Industrial Park
> Scranton, Pa. 18512

Apple II series; Commodore 64
Children build a train set by using keys or a joystock and then watch the trains run.

## LEARNING ACTIVITIES

1. Observe your children building with unit blocks. Which ones have reached the meaning stage in which they build representational buildings? How do these children do with computer programs?

2. Read a book about opposites to a small group of children and ask them what kinds of opposite actions they have seen Stickybear doing.

3. Observe children using *Stickybear Shapes* (or a similar shapes program) and note how long each child plays the game. What happens with the partner when one child plays for a long period?

4. Write down or tape record the questions or directions children give one another while at the computer. What does this tell you about the children's understanding of the concepts involved?

5. What evidence can you gather that the children have learned any of the concepts from the programs? That they know the rules for the programs? That their attention span is longer?

# The Computer as a Crayon

W hen young children first use a crayon on a piece of paper, they tend to cover the paper with an endless series of continuous lines. It is a purely muscular production, often quite rhythmic in nature as they move the crayon back and forth or around and around. They are definitely manipulating the medium and have little interest in the marks their crayon is producing. In fact, they are not really watching what is happening. Later, as they become more aware of what the crayon is doing, their scribbles become more diverse and less continuous.

Rhoda Kellogg, who has analyzed young children's scribblings from around the world, has categorized the dots, lines, zigzags, loops, and circles into twenty basic scribbles. Children around the world seem to produce the same basic scribbles during the exploration period of their drawing skills development. Not every child scribbles all twenty designs; individuals tend to favor certain scribbles and to repeat them again and again, often one on top of another (Kellogg 1969).

Eventually, the scribbles become more simplified and shapelike. Young children seem to produce five basic shapes plus a miscellaneous form. The basic shapes include rectangle (including square), oval (including circle), Greek cross ( + ), diagonal cross (X), and an odd shape. Children then combine and recombine any of these six forms repeatedly during the manipulation period (Kellogg 1969).

From experimentation children eventually discover certain designs that are more pleasing than others: a cross on top of a circle, for instance. This design finally evolves into a sun, which in turn may be transformed into a person with arms and legs extending from its head-body. With more control over their drawing tool and a repertoire of shapes at their fingertips, children who have progressed through the stages of manipulation and experimentation begin to do representational drawing. As with block building,

**111**

they often do not name their designs until they are finished, for who knows when they start what the pictures will turn out to be?

## THE COMPUTER AS A CRAYON

The computer can also serve as a drawing tool for young children, the cursor being the crayon. There are many drawing programs available for preschool children. Some are easy to learn and use; others are difficult. Some programs use the keyboard for controlling the picture; others use external devices, such as a joystick, a mouse, a light pen, or a touch pad (see chapter 8). Just as children enjoy drawing and painting on paper, they enjoy drawing on the computer screen with their electronic crayon.

Children begin to draw on the computer by exploring how they can control the drawing. The program itself determines the stages of drawing children go through as they move from easy to difficult tasks. There are also limitations created by the computer itself. Computers vary in the type

*When children use drawing programs, they work more easily and enjoyably with a partner.*

of graphics and in the number of colors available. For instance, the Apple II series has two types of graphics: low-resolution graphics, which consist of small rectangles of color resembling tiny bricks; and high-resolution graphics, which consist of colored pixels. (A pixel is a dot on the screen.)

With its low-resolution graphics, the Apple II can provide fifteen colors (including black and white); with its high-resolution graphics, it can provide only six colors (including black and white). The Commodore 64 provides sixteen colors, which are available for all graphics applications including high-resolution programs. Perhaps the best way to illustrate the differences is a discussion in this chapter and the next of programs that use different approaches for screen drawing.

## EARLY GAMES FOR YOUNG CHILDREN: DRAW

The *Early Games for Young Children: Draw* is an example of a program that uses keyboard control for drawing. The child manipulates a low-resolution, colored cursor by striking the appropriate key. Keys on the top row move the cursor up, keys on the bottom row move it down, keys in the middle rows on the left of the keyboard move it left, keys in the middle rows on the right side move it right, and the keys in the corners are used to move the cursor diagonally that is, 1 moves the cursor up and to the left; -, up and to the right; Z, down and to the left; /, down and to the right). The space bar is used to change the color. Thus, key position is used to control the direction of the line in the drawing.

The advantage of this approach for the preschool program is that it uses the keyboard without requiring the child to memorize key commands. In most cases, striking a key in the proper section of the keyboard will move the drawing line in the desired direction. Children are thus able to induce the rules quite readily given the time and opportunity.

When *Draw* was introduced in the Elmira Project, children were told that there was a colored crayon (the cursor) on the screen that could be used by pressing the keys. They were also told that the color of the crayon could be changed by pressing the space bar. Children needed to look closely to find the crayon, for it started as a little pink dot. We tried both singles and partners with the drawing programs, but partners worked best. Regardless of the fact that children work alone when they draw with crayons and paper, they worked more easily and more enjoyably with a partner when using computer programs.

Whitney and Kathy were the first partners on the board. They found the pink dot without any trouble and began pressing the keys to see what would happen. The dot began drawing by moving one space at a time. At first, the children did not understand that they needed to continue pressing a key in order to keep the colored line going. Then Whitney said: "Want to change the color, Kathy? You push the space bar." The partners tried a number of color changes.

We noted that all of the operators tended to press keys in the same area of the keyboard at first. The cursor would make a line in one direction until it reached the edge of the screen and stopped. At this point, the children had to experiment until they discovered another section of the keyboard that moved the cursor in a different direction. If they backed over the line they had just created, the new line would blend into the previous line, and they would lose sight of the cursor. This seemed to be the most distracting problem with drawing programs controlled by keys.

Finally, children learned they could always find their "lost" crayon by changing its color. Pushing the space bar caused a different color dot to show up in the drawing line, and the child would be able to locate the end of the crayon once again.

Diagonal movements were the last to be discovered by the children, probably because these lines were controlled by a smaller number of keys than horizontal and vertical line movement. Also, these particular keys were in the corners of the keyboard and not in the central section that children used more frequently.

Erasing a line was also puzzling. The only way to erase in *Draw* is to choose the black crayon and move it back over the line to be erased. None of the children discovered this strategy. But, it really is not needed by preschoolers who are not as concerned with their final product as older children might be. Young children, after all, are not drawing a picture at this stage but are manipulating the medium to see what can be done with it. Even when they reach the level of representational drawing, they tend not to erase but to incorporate everything they have drawn into their picture. Erasing the entire picture by accident and having to start over are other problems altogether and will be discussed later.

When children tried to press several keys with more than one finger, the cursor tended to go in one direction more than another until it came to the end of the line. Then the operators were stuck. We suggested that each partner use only one computer finger and observe the direction in which their electronic crayon went. Although a few children went back to pushing the cursor keys, which they had used most recently in *Stickybear Opposites* and *Shapes*, most soon realized that it was not particular keys they needed to use, rather particular locations on the keyboard.

Once a small group of experts has emerged, the best instructional strategy is to have an experienced drawer operate the board with an inexperienced partner. The children not only made excellent instructors, but also developed mastery and creativity through their partnerships.

## STAGES IN USING DRAW

As with other programs, children progress through three learning stages. Those are manipulation, mastery, and meaning.

### Manipulation

During manipulation, the children explored the capabilities of the program, trying out different keys and colors. One of the girls discovered how to fill the designs with color by drawing parallel lines with no space between them. The children also learned that to draw a line, they had to press one key until the line was the desired length. Children first tried pressing a different key every time. This resulted in a tiny compressed design: a little bunch of colors. Some children understood how to operate the program immediately. Others needed help from their partners. Still others pushed only one key and waited. When nothing else happened, they gave up and left.

### Mastery

During mastery the children learned how to make squares, rectangles, stairs (diagonal lines), and on the Apple II to avoid the RESET and ESCAPE keys unless they wanted to start over. Nick made this discovery by accident. He drew lines, stairs, and changed colors several times. Then he accidentally pressed ESCAPE, and the program started from the beginning with the moving menu. He had to wait for each program icon (symbol) to appear on the screen before the icon for *Draw* appeared. Then he had to press the space bar quickly before the menu changed in order to start the drawing program. He missed his chance the first time and had to go through the menu again. Although an adult might be annoyed by the delay, children treat moving menus as a game to be played until they win (that is, press the space bar in time to catch *Draw*).

TJ soon learned how to draw long lines in the direction he wanted. "I think I'll make the garage," he declared and made both a house and a garage. Then he accidentally pressed the RESET key but did not let it bother him, even though his drawing had been erased. "I made the wrong thing I wanted to do," he said to his partner and then pressed RESET every time he moved his crayon in the wrong direction. Finally, he decided that his drawing was starting to look like a house.

As the children progressed and discovered new ways to draw, mastery increased. The children at the computer began to discuss what they wanted to build and which keys they needed to use. In the Elmira Project, the children from the three-year-old group mastered the program more rapidly than the four year olds. They were calmer, more disciplined, and showed greater tolerance when they did not understand the program.

## Meaning

During the meaning stage, the children began naming the geometric shapes they had created and then started making up stories about them. "Is that a house?" asked a child after one of her partners had drawn two stacked rectangles. "And here is the basement," was the reply as the partner pointed to the lower rectangle. Then they inserted a diagonal line for stairs and added a smaller rectangle on the side for a garage. Because rectangles and diagonal stairs are so easy to make with this program, the first representational figure is usually a house. One child made the house, the stairs, and then "a way out in case there is a fire."

## WHAT CHILDREN LEARNED FROM DRAW

As the children gained greater mastery, they learned how to predict the size of the shape they were making, how to make solid shapes by coloring with lines that touched each other, and how to work together at a common task. The social interaction at this stage is similar to group play in which children work together to build a garage in the block corner.

As children gain control over the program, they begin to concentrate on incorporating the images into a story or game, rather than worrying about the mechanics of building the images. Just as some children take only one crayon from the box, and others are so fascinated with color that they use every crayon, so there is variation in the use of color with *Draw*. Some children try to put all of the colors into one line, while others concentrate on shapes and change colors only when they are encouraged to do so. Children seem to recognize the various colors without difficulty, and one partner always seems able to name even the lightest and darkest shades—another learning experience afforded by programs like this.

## ACTIVITIES TO BE USED WITH COMPUTER DRAWING PROGRAMS

With each of the computer programs we introduced, we also brought into the classroom a corresponding game, activity, or toy to help children understand the program or give them a chance to apply their computer learning to activities in the classroom. Drawing geometric designs on a screen by means of keys that control the drawing implement reminded us of the commercial toy Etch-a-Sketch. We decided to integrate computer drawing into the curriculum by bringing in a real Etch-a-Sketch. The children were excited with this new toy and wanted to use it as much as they did the computer. We placed it on a table near the computer corner for children to use while they waited for a turn at the computer. Most children merely played around with it, but a few made designs that they named.

The teachers also had crayons and felt-tipped markers available (as they do throughout the year) during the weeks that *Draw* was being used. Other appropriate kinds of drawing might include: colored chalk and chalkboard, finger paints, glue drawings on colored paper, squeeze-bottle drawings, and salt drawings in which designs are made with a finger on a salt-covered tray and then erased by shaking.

Books have a place in the early childhood curriculum to help motivate particular activities. Any of the small format books featuring Harold and his purple crayon are appropriate. Crocket Johnson's *A Picture for Harold's Room* (New York: Scholastic Book Services, 1960) shows Harold drawing a little town with houses, a road, hills, the ocean, a train track, and a bird, all of which get larger as he goes along. Preschoolers do not understand perspective in art, but they love the *Harold* books anyway.

Jack Kent's *The Scribble Monster* (New York: Harcourt, Brace, Jovanovich, 1981) is a wordless picture book about a boy and girl who draw graffiti that comes to life.

## LOGO TURTLE GRAPHICS FOR PRESCHOOL CHILDREN

Another approach to drawing with the keyboard can be found in programs that are modeled after LOGO turtle graphics. LOGO is a computer language developed by the Massachusetts Institute of Technology's Artificial Intelligence Project. The project included extensive work teaching computer programming to elementary school children.

While LOGO is a high-level language with commands to manipulate words and lists, most people associate LOGO with on-screen graphics. In fact, most literature about LOGO and young children equates LOGO with turtle graphics. The name *turtle graphics* comes from a project in which the children programmed a turtle-shaped robot to draw pictures on a large piece of paper using a ball-point pen in the turtle's belly. Directions that control the turtle consist of commands, such as FORWARD 100 (move forward 100 steps), RIGHT 90 (turn right 90 degrees) and LEFT 45 (turn left forty-five degrees). In learning to control the turtle, children in the elementary grades learn intuitively the concepts of distance and degrees as well as other concepts of arithmetic and geometry. On the computer screen, the turtle is represented by the cursor.

One strategy for learning to program the turtle is to have one child pretend to be the turtle while the other children give commands to the "turtle" to determine whether their commands will work. The influence of Papert's classic book about this project, *Mindstorms*, and the availability of LOGO for personal computers have made LOGO turtle graphics a model for many children's computer drawing programs.

## YOUNG CHILDREN'S USE OF LOGO

Programs based on LOGO that are appropriate for preschool children have a triangular cursor on the screen, a screen turtle. Examples of drawing programs based on turtle graphics include *Delta Drawing* and other forms of minimal or instant LOGO (see software at the end of this chapter). In minimal or instant LOGO, the commands for programming words are missing, and the drawing commands normally consist of single letters that correspond to a preset distance or turning radius. For example, a command of F would move the turtle forward two steps, and a command of L would turn the turtle thirty degrees to the left. Each time the single-letter command is given, the turtle cursor moves, leaving a trail (line) behind it.

Single-letter control is well within the capacity of children between the ages of three and five. However, these programs using turtle-graphic commands, while based on LOGO, are not LOGO. LOGO involves a level of literacy beyond the abilities of most young children. Programming with full implementation of LOGO is probably not practical for children before second grade. It is possible, however, for children with a strong background in minimal LOGO to write simple LOGO programs by the second semester of the first grade. (Clements 1983–1984, 24–29). Other projects have had some success with five-year-old children doing simple programming tasks in LOGO at the end of a concentrated training program (Hines 1983, 10–12).

## TURTLE COMMANDS AND DIRECTIONALITY

There are some aspects of turtle-graphic commands that can be very confusing to preschool children. Many preschoolers have trouble with the concepts of left and right and with spatial relationships because of their cognitive immaturity. To make a square with turtle graphics they must command the turtle to turn ninety degrees in the same direction three times. If the turtle is turning right, it turns to the child's right at the first command, it turns downward at the second command, and it turns to the child's left at the third command. These seemingly strange directions can confuse the preschool child, who has not yet learned directionality. Thus, if you plan to use a form of turtle graphics, it might be wise not to identify the R command as right and the L command as left when introducing the program.

Having children physically act out the drawings they want to make is well worth a try. It can be done with games such as Simon Says, or Turtle Says, if you enter fully into the spirit of turtle graphics. Turtle Says is an excellent strategy not only for visualizing the turtle commands, but also for teaching the concepts of forward, backward, right, and left. The concept of degrees is beyond preschool children, but they can be taught to turn "a little" (about thirty degrees) or "a lot" (ninety degrees). Most minimal LOGO programs use this strategy for turning the turtle. Because LOGO is so widely used in the elementary school curriculum, Turtle Says has, in fact, become a playground game in many parts of the country.

It is possible to obtain a turtle robot similar to the one originally used in the M.I.T. study. Although the price of a turtle is probably beyond the budget of most preschools, it might be possible to locate one at a local university or school district for a classroom demonstration. After learning basic turtle-graphic commands, the children can give the computer directions for the turtle to move any way they want. In the process, they will also learn additional commands, such as PEN UP, PEN DOWN, and PEN COLOR, which are part of the turtle-graphic set of commands.

While most minimal LOGO programs have no provision for delayed programming of the commands, *Delta Drawing* keeps track of the keyboard commands and has a provision for storing a sequence of commands. Children who become experts at using the commands may be able to use this feature to create a simple drawing program.

Although it is fashionable to use LOGO as a primary instrument for computer literacy with children, it is probably not practical to use programs based on LOGO graphics with preschool children until they are totally comfortable with the computer keyboard and have worked with programs that involve sequential letter commands (see chapter 9). In the Elmira Project, we chose to use the simpler program, *Draw*, rather than the minimal LOGO program, *Delta Drawing*, because children could learn more easily how to control the cursor. Our goal was for children to learn to draw independently by abstracting the rules for a program through experimentation. With minimal LOGO programs, they need to memorize prescribed commands or refer to illustrated commands first, a difficult chore for preliterate children.

## PATTERN DRAWING PROGRAMS— IMAGINATION: QUILT

*Imagination: Quilt* represents another approach to keyboard commands for creating patterns on the screen. The bottom quarter of the screen has a menu of single-letter commands used to control the drawing. On the right side of the menu are the eight keys used to create the design. The letter I moves the cursor up, M moves the cursor down, J moves it right, and K moves it left. Diagonal movements are made with the U,O,N, and < keys. The children can be taught these keys to begin drawing. When they become competent with line drawings, they can move to the color menu.

Color choices are on the top line of the menu with a number under each color. Pushing the associated number key will change the color of the crayon on the screen. The next stage is to create a quilt with the pattern on the screen. The P(LAY) key slowly repeats the pattern in a different position until the space bar is pressed, stopping the picture. This process of repetition is known in computer programming as recursion.

Recursion is an important concept in computer programming because it involves designing a procedure that repeats itself. Perhaps the best example of recursion is the classic fairytale of "capturing a leprechaun." According to folk wisdom, when a leprechaun is captured three wishes are granted. After the first two wishes are used, what should the third wish be? According to the principle of recursion, the third wish should always be three more wishes!

Although the developers of *Quilt* have tested their program with children as young as three, *Quilt* should be used with children who have mastered the keyboard with programs such as *Stickybear ABC* and *Stickybear Numbers*. The ability to locate the letters and numbers quickly on the keyboard is necessary to avoid frustration. For the young child, one of the advantages of *Quilt* is that the cursor keys are clustered in one small section of the keyboard. The menu showing how the cursor keys are used is located on the monitor right above the keys themselves. Young children seem to like to work in a small, defined area of the keyboard.

One danger (or perhaps discovery opportunity) of key placement is that the P(LAY) key is located next to one of the drawing keys; thus, the repetition of the design can be accidentally triggered by pressing P instead of O. The B(RING) key is also next to the N cursor control key. If B is accidentally pressed, subsequently pressing one of the cursor control keys will move the entire design in the direction controlled by that key rather than draw a new dot. These problems are not serious, but they may surprise children during the exploration process.

*Quilt* has disk utilities and printer commands built into the program. Because they can damage the disk or stop the execution of the program if a printer is not connected to the computer, the commands are difficult to reach accidentally. The menu of commands requires using the shift key in combination with the + (plus) key. The utilities allow the teaching staff to create a new program disk, to save designs to disk or retrieve them from disk, and to create a storage disk. The utilities are not used by preschool children, but they are useful to older users.

Incidentally, *Quilt* is one of the few programs that allows the user to make copies. Most educational programs use elaborate protection schemes to prevent copying. It is particularly important that buyers use the copies to protect their original programs from damage and not abuse the privilege of being able to make copies by giving them away. Disks do wear out or become damaged, and it is important to have a supply of replacement programs with a minimum of trouble and expense.

One of the advantages of command-controlled programs, such as *Quilt* is that the program can grow with the child's increased computer competency. It is difficult to outgrow the program because new possibilities emerge with increasing skills. The excellent documentation that comes with *Quilt* contains suggestions for teaching the program to various age groups as well as how to design advanced projects. This flexibility is an important consideration for public schools and families making software purchases.

For the preliterate child, the important consideration for using this type of program is improving mastery and control over the machine, in addition to the pride that comes from creating aesthetically pleasing designs. Teachers may want to print out or save on disk a series of pattern drawings that individual children have created as evidence of their developing creativity and understanding of cognitive concepts.

## OBSERVING CHILDREN USING DRAWING PROGRAMS

It is important while observing children using drawing programs to determine what stage of learning they are in. Have they passed through the manipulation stage to mastery? What evidence do you have to make this determination? Observe how children use the keys. Do they press one at a time? Do they continue pressing the same key to keep their line going as far as they want? Do they still experiment with different keys, or do they seem to know which keys make the cursor go in the direction they want? Can they make diagonal lines easily? What about changing colors?

You also need to listen to what partners say to one another about their drawings to determine whether they have reached the meaning stage. Do they name their designs? Do they make up stories about them? Do they announce what they are going to do next and then do it? How is turn taking regulated? Does one partner do most of the drawing while the other one watches, or do they each add to the drawing?

Have the children begun to integrate skills learned from drawing programs with other art materials in the classroom? If you keep individual records of the children, check to see how far children have progressed in other drawing activities (for example, see if they scribble, draw shapes, or draw humans) and then compare that progress with their computer drawings.

## REFERENCES

**Beaty, Janice J.** *Observing Development of the Young Child.* Columbus, Ohio: Merrill Publishing Co., 1986.

**Clements, Douglas H.** "Supporting Young Children's LOGO Programming." *The Computer Teacher,* (December–January 1983–1984): 24–31.

**Cron, Mary.** "Spinnaker's Learning Games." *Popular Computing,* (August 1983): 196–200.

**Eyster, Richard H.** "Seymour Papert and the LOGO Universe." *Creative Computing,* (1983): 70–74.

**Haskell, Lendall L.** *Art in the Early Childhood Years.* Columbus, Ohio: Charles E. Merrill Publishing Co., 1979.

**Hines, Sandra N.** "Computer Programming Abilities of Five-Year-Old Children." *Educational Computer,* (July–August 1983): 10–12.

**Kellogg, Rhoda.** *Analyzing Children's Art.* Palo Alto, Calif.: National Press Books, 1970.

**Klink-Zeitz, Kathryn.** "Early Games for Young Children." *Personal Computer Age,* (1983): 73–74.

**Lough, Tom.** "Exploring New Horizons with LOGO: How One School is Charting the Course." *Electronic Learning,* (April 1983): 71–75.

**Murphy, Brian J.** "Educational Programs for the Very Young." *Creative Computing,* (October 1983): 107–18.

**Papert, Seymour.** *Mindstorms: Children, Computers, and Powerful Ideas.* New York: Basic Books, 1980.

**Schnatmeier, Vanessa.** "Dr. LOGO: A New Start for Beginners." *PC Magazine,* (March 1983): 422–29.

**Watt, Dan.** "LOGO: What Makes It Exciting?" *Popular Computing,* (August 1983): 106–12.

## SOFTWARE

*Delta Drawing*
> Spinnaker Software
> 215 First Street
> Cambridge, Mass. 02142

Apple II family, 48K, DOS 3.3, disk drive; Commodore 64, cartridge; IBM PC, memory required, 64K; PCjr, 64K, color graphics card; Atari 400, 800, all XL's

Discussed in this chapter. (Grades K and up)

*Discover!*
> Daybreak Software
> Div. of Educational Activities
> 1937 Grand Ave.
> Baldwin, N.Y. 11510

Apple II family; Commodore 64; IBM PC, memory required

Follows the philosophy of LOGO; preschoolers can discover concepts and develop basic skills.

*Early Games for Young Children: Draw*
> Springboard Software, Inc.
> 7807 Creekridge Circle
> Minneapolis, Minn. 55435

Apple II family, disk drive; Commodore 64; IBM PC; VIC-20; TRS-80 Model I, III, color computer; Atari

Discussed in this chapter. (Grades preschool–1)

*Early LOGO Learning Fun*
> Texas Instruments
> P. O. Box 2909, MS 2222
> Austin, Tex. 78769

TI home computer, ROM cartridge

Preschool children learn to use LOGO.

*EZ LOGO*
> MECC
> 3490 Lexington Ave. N
> St. Paul, Minn. 55112

Apple II family, DOS 3.3, 64K

Children learn to use LOGO in self-directed manner using one-letter commands.

*Imagination: Quilt*
> Wiley Professional Software
> John Wiley & Sons
> 605 Third Ave.
> New York, N.Y. 10158

Apple II family

Discussed in this chapter. (Grades K–6)

*Mindplay: Picture Perfect*
>Methods and Solutions
>300 Unicorn Park Dr.
>Woburn, Mass. 01801

Apple II family; Franklin Ace; IBM; 48K; 1984
Children use imagination with colors, shapes, and designs.

*Turtle Toyland, Jr.*
>Childware Corp./ HesWare
>150 North Hill Drive
>Brisbane, Calif. 94005

Commodore 64, joystick
A self-teaching program in which children select options such as "Playground," "Training Land," "Music Land," "Sprite Land," or "Toybox" with a joystick. Children build on experience with previous games as they learn to move the turtle around the screen, create designs, make music, design movable shapes, and finally put everything they have created together.

## LEARNING ACTIVITIES

1. Observe your children while they use a computer drawing program. Determine their learning on the basis of your observational data.

2. What stories do your children tell about the computer drawings they make? Record these stories on running records or the tape recorder.

3. Provide the children with a drawing activity, such as Etch-a-Sketch or some other new drawing activity. How do the children who use it compare with those who don't, on the basis of their computer drawings?

4. Observe your children drawing with the computer. Make a list of the things you feel they have learned as exhibited by their skill in drawing. Include conversational skills, computer literacy, concepts, social skills, and art skills.

5. Read one of the suggested books or a similar book to motivate your children to draw. Record the results.

# The Computer as a Paintbrush

Young children interact with painting materials in an entirely different manner than older children or adults. Many of them are highly attracted to paints and brushes. They want to get a brush in their hand and do something with it. In the beginning, that something is not necessarily a creative product. Children only want to manipulate the medium, as we have discussed in each of the previous chapters. They try out the medium, experiment with it, explore it, get control of it. If the "it" happens to be nothing more than water and a brush, young children are not a bit dismayed. They plunge in happily and paint the wall or the car or the sidewalk with water.

Adults are often puzzled by this activity. Why should children be so excited about putting water on something? It doesn't really accomplish anything, and, in the end, the water will only dry up and leave the surface as it was before. Wouldn't children rather use paint? No. Young children see no incongruity in painting with water. The results to them are inconsequential. They are not cognitively aware that the water will dry up and disappear. Even if they were, it probably would not matter. The process itself is most important.

Painting is a very physical activity, a rhythmical activity. One can express emotions through the physical act of painting something. A person can slap on paint or smooth it on or swish it as the mood dictates. In the end, the act of painting becomes a very personal expression.

What young children find intriguing is the act, not the product. In fact, the biggest misunderstanding that adults harbor with regard to young children's art is that it should turn out to be something. Children, unlike adults, are not as impressed by the product—the results of painting as they are by the process—the act of painting. Adults want something tangible from children's painting experiences: something nice to talk about, exclaim over, and send home to mother. Teachers and parents of preschoolers need to realize that young children will not produce finished products or even acceptable paintings during the early experimental stages. Instead, they will explore the medium to see what it will do and what they can do with it.

## PAINTING, DRAWING, AND COLOR

Painting is different from drawing whether it is done with a brush, a finger, or a computer joystick. While drawing is concerned with lines and shapes, painting is more fluid in terms of the tools used and the medium itself. Color also seems to play a more important role in painting than it does in drawing, and young children spend a great deal of time trying out colors: moving them around, mixing them, layering them on top of one another.

Children play with painting for the same reason they play with drawing: to find out how it works. Manipulation during their natural acquisition of painting skills is more physical than cognitive. Children explore the many ways a brush or a finger or a joystick can move colors around. They also hold their painting tool in different positions or with different hands to gain optimum control over it. Then they practice using it over and over.

Colors do not matter so much at first. Young children use whatever color is at hand. They are exploring the medium and not painting a picture. Young children's use of certain colors is related more to physical availability of the colors than anything else (Lowenfeld and Brittain 1975). In other words, they tend to use the paint that is closest to their brush hand. Observers have also noted that young children tend to use colors in the same order that they are placed on an easel tray.

Children progress through stages in learning to paint that are similar to those for drawing (see chapter 7). What is fascinating about the process is that a child does not necessarily go through the stages simultaneously, even when both activities are given equal time and opportunity. Quite often, children who have advanced from the scribble stage in drawing will still be scribbling in their painting (Lasky and Mukerji 1980, 50).

Once children have learned to handle a brush and colors and have practiced their skills until they gain control, they may begin to do representational painting. Although much of their work is original, some is based on what they see their peers making. While children do not really copy drawings, they may copy ideas. A favorite design during the latter preschool years is what the children call a rainbow: a bow of one color above another until all the available colors have been used. Some children seem to stumble on this design automatically, while others see peers doing it and try it for themselves.

The houses, humans, animals, and trees that young children eventually put in their drawings may look alike, but this is not because the children have copied one another. Instead, the designs children create look similar because they have emerged from a similar process. As children gain mastery, they gain originality in ideas and their execution.

## THE COMPUTER AS A PAINTBRUSH

Is the computer an appropriate instrument with which young children can explore painting and develop creativity? We think so. As with other activities in the preschool curriculum, painting can be explored on the computer screen by young partners. Children can learn to handle computer "brushes," and playfully explore the high- and low-resolution color palettes. Yet, many early childhood educators feel that computer programs are too stilted and mechanical to allow creativity. Can such programs really give children the freedom of a brush and paints?

Computer painting programs allow their users as much freedom as do easels or pallets. While drawing programs are confined to geometric shapes, painting programs allow children the freedom to swish or daub or swirl colors around the screen and to compose representational drawings. Such programs are as open to creativity as an easel and a paint box.

The colors available to your child painters depend on the kind of computer they are using as well as the program itself. For example, the Apple II series provides fifteen colors in low-resolution and six colors in high-resolution graphics (see chapter 7). Having more colors is not necessarily better for preschoolers. Three- and four-year-old children are just beginning to acquire art skills. Simpler is always better for beginners, who do not need a full range of colors to start. Many three year olds, and some four year olds, are just starting to recognize colors. They cannot identify or name more than a handful of colors. Three or four colors at a time are all they can comfortably handle.

For these reasons the Elmira Project utilized a simple painting program, *Learning with Leeper: Paint*. Only four colors are available to children from a "paint pot" in each corner of the screen: green, blue, violet and orange. Children spend more time manipulating the paintbrush (cursor) around the screen with a joystick than they do selecting a particular color. Much of their selection, in fact, is entirely accidental as they manuever the paintbrush around the screen, unintentionally touch a paint pot, and change the color of their brush.

## TOOLS FOR COMPUTER PAINTING

There is such a wide array of hardware to accompany painting programs that it seems worthwhile to discuss some of it in detail. Many of the tools are given further consideration in the software and hardware list at the end of the chapter.

## Touch Pad

While *Early Games for Young Children: Draw* and turtle-graphics programs use the keyboard to control drawing, many painting programs use an electronic "pallet" for controlling shapes, lines, and colors. An example of an electronic pallet is a touch pad, such as the Koala Touch Pad or the larger Power Pad. A touch pad is a thin, flat rectangular box with its own screen (pad) on top. The Power Pad is about the same size as the computer monitor. Such pads are connected to the computer by a cord that plugs into the joystick port.

Touch pads allow children to draw on the pad itself with a stylus. As they draw, their marks are duplicated on the screen. This feature allows freehand drawing on the computer screen. The software supplied with the touch pad includes a menu for shapes, colors, filling in shapes with colors, and drawing. Use of the menu by preschool children requires some instruction from the teacher. Touch pads are available for under $100 for both the pad and software. These electronic pallets are generally easy for young children to use.

Touch pads do present some disadvantages, however. First, touch pads normally require a stylus. Styluses can be hazardous to young children because they are small, rigid sticks like pencils. Small children may also try to draw on the touch pad with pencils, crayons, or other writing materials. We discovered it is virtually impossible to remove ball-point ink from a Chalkboard Power pad. Fingers can be used as a stylus, but they are not as precise and predictable as the stylus itself. Second, although thin lines are easy for small children to draw, using preprogrammed colors and shapes requires going back and forth from the menu to the picture by pressing a button on the top of the touch pad or touching the menu-selection area of the touch pad.

## Light Pen

A light pen looks like a black ball-point pen with the point retracted and has a cord for connecting it to the computer. With a light pen, a child can paint electronic pictures directly on the computer monitor. Light pens, such as the Gibson Light Pen by Koala Technologies, provide a way for the child to paint by pointing the pen toward the colors on the screen and then touching an area of the drawing to be filled in with that color. The pen must be held squarely against the monitor or TV screen. The pen's plastic housing protects the optical sensors in the light pen and screen. A light pen appears to be the most desirable instrument for painting. However, light pens have limitations that may be frustrating to the child.

The light pen must be moved slowly so that it has time to read the screen. Occasionally, the light pen does not read the screen accurately, either because of poor contrast on the screen, distortion from the plastic guard, or because the pen has been moved too quickly across the screen. These limitations can be frustrating for adults as well as young children. Light pens work better with color monitors than with monochromatic monitors. As light pen technology improves, these pens may be the optimum paintbrush for the preschool child, but they presently require more patience and careful use than many preschoolers can muster.

## Mouse

The mouse represents still another painting device for the computer. A mouse is a separate cursor-control device that rolls on a flat surface. It is called a mouse because it looks something like a mouse with buttons (eyes) at the front end and the cord (tail) at the back end connecting it to the computer.

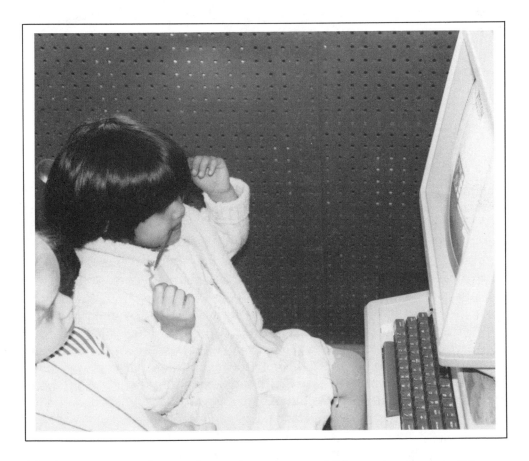

*The best way to evaluate software is to observe children using the program.*

The mouse has been popularized through the *MacDraw* program written for the Apple Macintosh. The features of this program have been incorporated into programs for other computers, such as *Mouse Paint* for the Apple II, *PC Paintbrush* for IBM PCs, and *GEM-paint* for computers using the GEM system. While the Macintosh paints only in black and white, the other programs use color.

Guiding the mouse on a flat surface allows the user to point to choices that include: freehand drawing, defined shapes, colors, and patterns, which are chosen by clicking a button on the mouse. Painting on the monitor is accomplished by holding the button down as the mouse is moved on a flat surface, such as a desktop. As long as the button is held down, the cursor paints a trail of color or a black line on the screen following the movements made by the mouse.

The mouse requires that the user be able to guide it and hold down the button at the same time. Children under three find this a difficult or impossible task because their hands are not large enough. Children over 3½ years old seem to have little trouble using a mouse, if they have a large enough surface on which to move the mouse. Using the mouse on a smaller surface takes greater skill. The mouse is standard equipment with some of the newer computers, such as the Apple Macintosh or the Commodore Amiga. It is an option costing $100 or more for the Apple II series or IBM-compatible computers. It is not available for all brands of home computers.

## Joystick

The most common paintbrush for small computers is the joystick. Joysticks are small hand-held boxes with button(s) and a short control stick on top. They are operated by rotating the stick, which moves the cursor on the computer screen. They are relatively inexpensive ($30-$60) and most personal computers come with a joystick port for hooking up the device. Thus, joysticks have become one of the most popular computer attachments for painting programs.

Although many preschool children use and enjoy joysticks, they can pose some difficulties. For instance, the joystick orientation may not correspond directly to cursor movement. If the joystick box happens to be turned around, then the cursor will not move in the same direction in which the joystick is pushed. A more difficult problem is that the joystick can be moved faster than the cursor. Until a high level of skill is reached, it is difficult to move the cursor with precision using a joystick. Results can be unexpected when the cursor moves farther than the user intended. Such roadblocks can transform a potentially exciting program into a frustrating experience (see chapter 10).

A problem with most external devices (joysticks, touch pads, light pens, and the mouse) is that only one child at a time can use them. Although it is easy to share a keyboard, it is difficult to share a joystick. Passing the joystick back and forth does not always work well because the joystick's orientation may change. Young partners also have more difficulty sharing a joystick than sharing the keyboard, and squabbles will arise.

It is probably wise to restrict the use of joysticks and other external devices to one child at a time. Such restriction, though, makes this kind of computer painting less attractive than keyboard-controlled art. Children enjoy social contact at the computer. Their attention span is longer when they can share their creativity with others.

## Paddles

One of the oldest (and least satisfactory) external control device is the game paddle. Game paddles usually come in sets of two. They each consist of a knob on top of a rectangular box with one button on the side. One paddle moves the cursor up and down, and the other paddle moves the cursor side to side. Manipulating them simultaneously produces diagonal movement. The paddles are connected by a cord that plugs into the joystick port. The knobs on the paddles draw in a manner similar to that of an Etch-a-Sketch. Drawing with paddles requires a great degree of concentration and coordination. Paddles can be used for collaborative drawing with one child controlling the vertical paddle while the other controls the horizontal paddle. However, such an arrangement may lead to power struggles over the direction of the line. Most computer owners prefer using a joystick (which combines the functions of the two paddles into one instrument) over game paddles as an external control device.

## Touch Screen

A device that may overcome the limitations of paddles, joysticks, touch pads, light pens, and the mouse is the touch screen. The touch screen is a transparent touch pad placed over the monitor screen. It is attached to the computer via the joystick port. The Touch Window by Personal Touch is available for the Apple II and other computers at $200 or less. Such a device allows the user to draw by moving a finger across the touch screen. Touching the screen also selects items from the menu. Children can take turns painting on the screen without having to pass a device back and forth. Such a screen also offers the advantage of a light pen by allowing children to paint or draw directly on the screen.

Still, there are several disadvantages for preschoolers. If young children become used to drawing on a touch screen, they may try to draw on the monitor when the touch screen is off. Furthermore, vertical surfaces are difficult for artists to use, especially beginning artists. The muscular development and eye-hand coordination necessary for success in painting call for a slanted surface like that of an easel.

## LEARNING WITH LEEPER

*Learning with Leeper is an* example of a painting program for preschool children that uses a joystick. The child selects the program by moving Leeper, a one-eyed being, to a spilled paint bucket on the menu. When Leeper reaches the paint bucket, the painting program is retrieved from the disk. After a brief demonstration in which Leeper paints a house with trees, the painting program appears on the screen.

The joystick controls an image of a paintbrush (the cursor), which leaves a trail of paint as it moves around the screen. In each corner are paint cans with different colors of spilled paint. As the brush passes over a paint can, the color of the brush's trail changes. If the child wishes to move the brush without painting, it is necessary to hold down one of the buttons on the joystick; pressing the other button will clear the picture and start the program over.

Children learn to control the joystick in a very short time. When using *Learning with Leeper,* children usually begin by moving the brush around the edges of the screen as they test the outside limits of the joystick, making a four-colored border around the screen as the brush passes through each color of paint. Next, they move diagonally across the screen. Then, they try smaller movements, the result being small wiggles in the line. Within about twenty minutes, the child gains control over the joystick and begins to make designs similar to those made with paints and easel.

One way to introduce the joystick for painting is with an Etch-a-Sketch. Children enjoy figuring out the Etch-a-Sketch, and it prepares them for understanding how the joystick works. In fact, drawing with the joystick is really much easier than creating pictures with the Etch-a-Sketch because the joystick combines the two control knobs into one.

When the joystick is introduced, the teacher needs to point out that the cord should always be away from the child and towards the computer. It is easy to make the mistake of holding the joystick with the cord sticking out to the side, thus changing its orientation and causing the cursor to move in unrelated directions.

## WHAT CHILDREN LEARN FROM PAINTING PROGRAMS

Children can exercise more freedom with computer painting programs than with most other computer games. Once they have learned to manage the joystick or other painting tool, they can move the cursor freely in any direction. Children can be more creative with their designs when they do not have to deal with the constraints imposed by geometric shapes. In addition to design creativity, children can experiment with colors and color concepts. As with drawing programs, children like to name designs and make up stories about their creations. Finally, using a cursor-control device gives young artists a great deal of practice with small-motor skills and eye-hand coordination.

Coloring book programs with predesigned pictures offer the same practice with perceptual and motor skills. (Examples are *Color Me and Colorasaurus.*) Children like them but teachers have serious reservations about their stereotyped pictures, just as they dislike actual coloring books in the classroom. Because of their interactive nature, computer programs should never be considered books. However you may want to preview coloring book programs to see what children actually do and how much they actually gain from them.

## METHODS FOR SAVING COMPUTER ART

At some point while using the computer for art activities, the children or teacher may want to save their art. There are various ways to save art. Some programs allow the art to be saved on disk for later retrieval. Programs may also provide for a printout on a dot-matrix printer with graphics capability. The major problem with most dot-matrix printers is that the picture will be in black and white. However, there are a few such printers that print in multiple colors.

Some studies suggest that children can copy their art using clear plastic sheets taped over the monitor. After the computer-generated picture is finished, the child traces it on the plastic sheet with crayons or felt-tipped pens that write on plastic (Alexander 1983, 6). There are, however, a number of problems using this approach with preschool children. There is the housekeeping problem of crayon residue falling into the keyboard. There is the fact that few preschoolers are skilled in copying designs. Even more serious is the problem of children coloring on and damaging the unprotected screen once they have learned to mark on a screenlike surface.

Another way to save screen paintings is with color photos. The room should be well lighted with no glare from lights, windows, or flashguns on the screen, and high-speed, color film should be used. Instant cameras without flash can be used for this purpose, although a 35-mm camera is more reliable.

When all of the options are weighed, the best approach to making copies of children's computer art for display may still be a printer. Making printouts gives children another opportunity to learn how computers work.

Saving children's computer art, however, is often of greater concern to adults than children. Because young children's real interest is in the process of painting rather than the product they have created, it is often teachers and parents who want to preserve their paintings. Watch children paint on the computer and you may notice that they take as much pleasure in erasing their product and starting over as they do in creating it.

Nevertheless, children's computer art is highly creative and often beautiful. It deserves to be displayed if that is what children want. It deserves to be saved if teachers and parents want to follow their children's art development over time. Saving art on computer disks seems to be the most reasonable solution at the moment. If saving computer art is your concern, you will want to purchase painting programs with save features. If displaying computer art is your main concern, you will want to purchase equipment with printing capability.

## INTEGRATING PAINTING PROGRAMS INTO THE CURRICULUM

Computer painting provides another medium for children to explore the elements of art: line, shape, and color. The various cursor-control devices also provide opportunities for improving eye-hand coordination as the child manipulates the image on the screen. While computer painting involves completely different tasks than computer alphabets or numbers, children learn to use these programs quickly. Children enjoy controlling the computer. They like to discover how the program works. The process of discovery leads to new skills and knowledge.

Using art programs on the computer can easily be related to other classroom art activities, such as the painting corner. As they do when painting, children on the computer make random shapes until their imagination discovers patterns in those shapes. They may draw lines in various colors and see a rainbow in the lines. They may crisscross the screen with lines and discover a jail. They may draw rectangles and find a house. This interplay between discovery and imagination makes any freehand art activity exciting for the young child. The screen is an electronic piece of paper and the moving cursor is an electronic paintbrush.

At the same time, be sure to keep your easels up. Have paints ready for children when they come in the morning. Easels are important in early childhood classrooms because they allow independence. No teachers need to be involved once the paints and paper are ready. If children have problems with runny paint, make the paint thicker when you mix it.

Other kinds of painting should also be available. Children enjoy finger painting with several colors at a time. Making hand- and footprints with paint not only shows children a different way to make designs on paper, it also promotes positive self-concept.

Besides hands-on painting activities, teachers should provide other classroom activities that explore painting. What better way to interest children than to read good books about other children's or animals' experiences with paints? Margaret Wise Brown's *The Color Kittens* (New York: Golden Press, 1977) is a classic children's book about Brush and Hush, kittens that start out using all the colors in the world in their painting but cannot make green until they discover it by accident.

Bill Martin, Jr. and Eric Carle's *Brown Bear, Brown Bear, What Do You See?* (New York: Holt, Rinehart and Winston, 1967) with its large, double-page spreads of colored animal pictures asks and answers questions about colors in rhyme. Don Freeman's *A Rainbow of My Own* (New York: Viking Press, 1966) shows a little boy who tries unsuccessfully to catch a rainbow but then imagines his own private rainbow and how he would play with it, until he finds a real rainbow of his very own. Arnold Spilka's *Paint All Kinds of Pictures* (New York: Scholastic Book Services, 1963) is a collection of pictures—big, small, scary, exciting—that a child could imagine painting.

## OBSERVING CHILDREN USING PAINTING PROGRAMS

Painting programs offer an opportunity to observe children creating art with a different medium. It is important for the teacher and staff to observe the child's use of this medium. Once children have passed the manipulative stage and seem to have mastered the computer as a paintbrush, you should observe to see whether they are at the same level of artistic development as they are at the painting easel. What similarities in artistic style do you observe? What differences? Do children stay with painting programs as long as they stay on the easel? Do they finish their designs or do they erase them and start over? What elements of the computer program hold their interest the longest?

As we know, young children are more concerned with the process than the product. Even those who have mastered the use of computer painting programs may prefer to push an ESCAPE key (or whatever it takes) and erase their markings only to start all over again. Etch-a-Sketch offers the same attractiveness: shaking it upside down erases the sketch. If easel art could be erased, we probably would have fewer children's paintings to decorate classroom walls!

How do children use colors in their computer artwork? Do colors seem to make a difference, or does the child use whatever is at hand? Do children talk about colors while creating their computer paintings? Do they try to find certain colors to represent certain things or ideas?

Be sure to observe and record what children say about their paintings. Do they name their configurations or make up stories about their pictures? Turn on the tape recorder and pick up children's comments about their work.

Young children's use of painting programs on the personal computer has only begun. Its future will depend not only on the programs and hardware available, but also on teacher support and encouragement of this new medium for creativity and child development.

## REFERENCES

**Alexander, David.** *Children's Computer Drawings.* ERIC Document, ED 238 562, 1983.

**Haskell, Lendall L.** *Art in the Early Childhood Years.* Columbus, Ohio: Charles E. Merrill Publishing Co., 1979.

**Lasky, Lila,** and **Rose Mukerji.** *Art: Basic for Young Children.* Washington, D.C.: National Association for the Education of Young Children, 1980.

**Lowenfeld, Viktor,** and **W. Lambert Brittain.** *Creative and Mental Growth.* New York: Macmillan, 1975.

## SOFTWARE AND HARDWARE

*Color Me*
> Versa Computing, Inc.
> 3541 Old Conejo Rd.
> Newbury Park, Calif. 91320

Apple II series, 48k, disk

*Colorasaurus*
> The Learning Company
> 545 Middlefield Rd., Suite 170
> Menlo Park, Calif. 94025

Atari 400, 800, XL series, BASIC cartridge required, 48k, disk

*Computer Palette*
> Edutek Corp.
> 415 Cambridge, No. 4
> P.O. Box 11354
> Palo Alto, Calif. 94306

Apple II series, disk, 32K, requires game paddles

*GEM-Paint*
> Digital Research
> 60 Garden Court
> Monterey, Calif. 93942

For computers using the GEM operating system.

*Learning with Leeper: Paint*
> Sierra On-Line, Inc.
> P.O. Box 485
> Coarsegold, Calif. 93614

Apple II series, requires joystick
(Grades preschool–1)

*MacPaint*
> Apple Computer, Inc.
> 20525 Mariani
> Cupertino, Calif. 95014

Apple Macintosh, requires mouse, black and white graphics
(Grades preschool and up)

*Micro Illustrator*
> Koala Technologies Corp.
> 3100 Patrick Henry Dr.
> Santa Clara, Calif. 95052-8100

Apple II; Commodore 64; possibly IBM PC, packaged with the Koala Touch Pad

*Mouse Paint*
> See *MacPaint*

Apple II series, requires mouse

*Paint*
> Reston Publishing Co.
> 11480 Sunset Hills
> Reston, Va. 22090

Atari 800 with monitor and joystick, 48K, disk

*Paint Brush*
> HesWare (Human Engineered Software)
> 150 N Hill Dr.
> Brisbane, Calif. 94005

Apple, Atari, Coleco, Commodore, IBM

*Pentrak*
> Koala Technologies Corp.
> 3100 Patrick Henry Dr.
> Santa Clara, Calif. 95050

Apple II series, packaged with the Gibson Light Pen

*Power Pad*
> Chalk Board, Inc.
> 5470D Oakbrook Parkway
> Norcross, Ga. 30093

Painting software bundled with the Power Pad touch pad

*Touch Window*
> Personal Touch
> San Jose, Calif.

Apple II series, IBM PC

## LEARNING ACTIVITIES

1. Observe several children using a computer painting program. What colors do they use most? What do they do with the colors? Do colors seem to matter to them? How can you tell?

2. Compare the easel artwork of three children with paintings they make on the computer. How are they alike or different?

3. Record what children say about their computer paintings. Do they name their designs? Do they make up stories about them?

4. Have one of your computer artists teach you how to use the painting program. From this experience, can you tell what the children have learned from computer painting?

5. Set up a new art experience for the children (something using paints or different colors). Which children really get involved? What do these same children do with art on the computer?

Chapter 9

# The Computer as a Chatterbox

J ust as young children learn to build with blocks or draw with crayons by experimenting with the materials, they also learn to talk by playing with words. Most adults are not aware that young children learn much of anything through play, therefore, they seldom pay attention to the playful way that children use new words and sounds. Repeating nonsense words, chanting, or mumbling while half-asleep is usually dismissed as an unimportant activity children engage in when they first start talking, just as they do with scribbling before they can draw or write.

Researchers who observe and record young children's acquisition of their native language know better. They have evidence that children love to play with language by experimenting with rhythms and cadences, by mixing up words to create new meanings, and by using dialogues, chants, and a variety of vocalizations as they "poke fun at the world" or "verify their grasp of reality" (Schwartz 1981, 16). Furthermore, these specialists understand that young children play with language in order to teach themselves how to use it.

Infants, toddlers, and preschoolers are surrounded by language. Parents, siblings, peers, the radio, television, and tape recorders fill their world with words. Most youngsters are encouraged to listen, to say the names of things, and to pronounce words correctly. But their primary mechanism for learning language is self-teaching. They do it by listening to and imitating people around them. As with all of their learning, young children induce the rules for talking and then apply them to a variety of situations. They experiment with words in all sorts of ways according to the rules they have subconsciously extracted hearing others speak. In so doing, they use words and sounds and language in wonderful and original ways.

Kornei Chukovsky, the dean of Russian children's writers, has said: "It seems to me that, beginning with the age of two, every child becomes for

*Working in pairs stimulates children's conversation.*

a short period of time a linguistic genius. Later, beginning with the age of five to six, this talent begins to fade. There is no trace left in the eight year old of this creativity with words, since the need has passed; by this age the child already has fully mastered the basic principles of his native language" (1968, 7).

## THE COMPUTER AS A CHATTERBOX

Can computer programs assist the nonliterate child with playful practice in using words? We have found that the computer learning center in the preschool classroom offers an unparalleled opportunity for children to use words on their own. Because children acquire language competence through interacting with people and things in their environment, the computer's interactive features make it a powerful language development tool. Certain programs can stimulate the use of new words, the expanded use of familiar words, and the making up of stories to go along with computer pictures.

It is not only the computer programs themselves, but also the chance to converse with a partner that encourages children to learn language while at the computer. When children use the keyboard together, they are forced to communicate. Consequently, we strongly urge all preschool programs to set up their computers for simultaneous use by at least two children.

## Promoting Conversation

From the outset of the Elmira Project, we noted that partners at the computer would communicate with one another as soon as they were comfortable with the program. Some of the first conversations, however, sounded more like self-talk than conversation directed toward a partner. For example, when Johanna first experimented with the mixed-up animals program *Jeepers Creatures,* she talked about what she was doing to no one in particular. "That's superdog!" she exclaimed about one mixed-up animal. "Is there any owl on here? How do you get the owl?"

*Computer programs can promote vocabulary development.*

No one listened to her, and she received no answer. Nor did she really seem to expect one. Several child psychologists have studied this so-called private speech in which many children engage and find it to be transitional between internal thought and verbalized speech (Berk 1985, 48). We realize that adults also talk to themselves on occasion, especially when they have a difficult or unusual problem to solve.

Johanna was trying to find out how to create whole, correct animals. She talked to herself as she worked. Then Eric joined her and happened to make a complete frog. "Let's see if we can get other animals like this," she said, still not quite sure how to do it. "Hit that key and see what happens," she directed. As they worked, Johanna's conversation ceased to be private and became directed toward Eric. When it became her turn, Johanna discovered that the top row of letter keys controlled the animal's head, the middle row the body, and the bottom row the feet. "If you hit the top row you get a head," she then communicated to Eric.

We noted that the conversations between partners often centered on whose turn it was. Turn-taking problems were frequently settled, in fact, through talking rather than through physical struggle as is so often the case with other favorite classroom toys or activities. Rossy was excited the third time he used the computer and suddenly discovered how to make a whole frog. "Hey, look what I found!" he exclaimed. "Let's see how many other animals we can make." Then it was Michael's turn to try and Rossy reluctantly encouraged him. How difficult to share something so new and exciting! But then the watching partner discovered that he or she could still participate with the acting partner through language.

In summary, the conversations between partners at the computer include:

1. Giving information

2. Giving directions

3. Asking questions

4. Answering questions

5. Settling turn-taking problems

6. Telling the partner what the operator plans to do next

7. Critiquing the partner's work

8. Making comments about the program

9. Making up games

10. Making exclamations

The Elmira Project was a revelation to us all when we remember how worried we were that the children would have no need for talking or peer interaction.

## Promoting Vocabulary Development

In addition to conversations between partners, computer programs can promote vocabulary development. In all of the programs that our children used, they were exposed to new vocabulary words, most of which were illustrated graphically. With *Jeepers Creatures* children learned to make a kangaroo, a panda, and an octopus, as well as the more common cat and dog. A tape-recorded conversation illustrates how three-year-old partners were exposed to new words as they operated the program:

> Child 1: Watch when I push these two buttons. (*Pushes three*)
>
> Child 2: Some kind of fish.
>
> Child 1: Did you get a giraffe?
>
> Child 2: I hate that. (*The mixed-up graphic*)
>
> Child 1: What about an alligator?

While using *Stickybear ABC*, the children frequently named the graphic that illustrated the particular letter. Even a 1½-year-old visitor named airplane and hat! Several children had not been familiar with volcano. "What's a volcano?" asked one partner. The other started to explain but pushed V and the graphic appeared. "Oh, that's a volcano," was the satisfied comment.

The teacher saw the children looking at the graphic for helicopter and wondered if they knew what it was. She asked them, "What's that?" "A helicopter," was the prompt reply. "What does it start with?" continued the teacher. "H," answered the child. "Good for you!" she exclaimed.

Children also made up their own words for the unfamiliar graphics. The satellite graphic in *Stickybear Numbers* was frequently called "flying saucer" or even the original and descriptive "space ball."

## Promoting Reading Skills

The concept of picture symbolization is at the core of most good computer programs for preliterate children. But to read, children eventually have to learn that words stand for names of things, that letters have a sound and a name, and that groups of letters make up certain words. Because preliterate children cannot yet read words, computer programs aimed at these children must present ideas in pictorial form. If the program uses written words or directions, an adult needs to read them to the children.

Occasionally, however, children who have extracted meaning from computer programs showing combinations of pictures and words will begin to display reading skills. For those children, *Jeepers Creatures* promotes reading skills. At the bottom of the screen is the name of the mixed-up animal that the children have created: catowlfish, for example. A few of our children realized that the long word represented a combination of three animal names and tried to sound out the word. Jeremey, for instance, became so involved in trying to decipher the crazy animal names that he let his partner completely control the keyboard during his turn. It was a marvelous discovery for him to crack the reading code. While it is not necessary or appropriate for every preschool child to learn to read such words, it is an additional challenge for children who have induced the rules for unscrambling the animal pictures, to apply their learning to the unscrambling of the mixed-up animal names as well.

## MAKING UP STORIES

Our primary interest in using the computer to promote preschoolers' language development centered around our search for programs that would encourage children to make up their own stories. With very few exceptions, we found that most story programs on the market contained written words and needed an adult to read the directions or to write the words. This sort of program did not let children learn how to use the programs independently.

The children themselves showed us what programs were best for encouraging made-up stories. What a surprise to find that drawing programs were among the best story programs for preschoolers! *Early Games: Draw* quickly became a favorite and attracted children to the computer area to see what was being created on the screen.

As with paper and paint drawings, three- and four-year-old children do not set out to make representational pictures on the computer. They are still at the manipulation stage. But as the colored lines begin to fill the screen, the partners are inevitably stimulated by the designs they have created to make some meaning of them. If they do not comment themselves, then onlookers are sure to make their own guesses.

"Is that a house?" one onlooker asked. After studying her abstract design, the keyboard operator, Kathy, finally declared, "This is the basement." "Mine's gonna be a better picture than yours," was the typical reply.

When Barbie Sue and Kyle began a drawing program, Barbie was tentative at first but then caught on and soon filled the screen with two large, multicolored rectangles adjacent to one another. Kyle wanted her to describe what she was drawing, but she wouldn't. Finally she declared, "It's a design." Kyle did not accept this and insisted, "You have to call it something. Are you making a house?" At last, Barbie Sue found meaning in her drawing and replied, "I'm making the inside of a house. This is the downstairs. This is the upstairs."

Most impressive was the fact that the children not only figured out how to use the program at one sitting, but also made up stories about their drawings from the start. Thus, manipulation, mastery, and meaning took place before our eyes in a very compressed amount of time.

## PROGRAMS THAT PROMOTE THE MAKING UP OF STORIES: FACEMAKER

Because most of the computer story-telling programs on the market used words and were more appropriate for literate children, we looked for interesting pictorial software that preschool children could use for pretending. We hoped that at the meaning level they would progress to making up stories for the pictures they had created. The first of such programs was another classic for the preliterate child, called *Facemaker*. It was by far the most complicated program we used and initially required adult assistance to learn the commands.

Nevertheless, our two groups of three and four year olds had less difficulty than novices might because of their five-week exposure to the computer. Later, we also used *Facemaker* with two three- and four-year-old novices and found that they too could operate the program independently after minimum assistance.

After the title graphic appeared, the program operator had to make several choices in response to word questions on the screen. Preliterate children needed an adult to read the questions in the beginning. Later, the children usually remembered enough about these word cues to answer yes or no on their own. The first question, for instance, was Do you want sound? Although children did not quite understand the implication of this question, we instructed them to answer yes. Later, they could try the program without sound and make up their own sounds.

The next question asked whether the operator wanted a white background. Preliterate children had no idea how a program would be affected by such a choice. Nor for that matter, did novice adults. A yes response elicited the black outline of a head against a white background; a no response brought up a white outline against a black screen. The face they would construct was just as interesting against white as black.

Once they had made these choices, four menu options appeared: (1) build, (2) program, (3) game, (4) choice. We instructed children to choose option one which builds a face. They later used option two to program their newly constructed face. Option three, a memory game, was an advanced level that most preschoolers did not reach without adult help. Option four brought the operator back to the original choices of sound, color, and menu.

For the build option, an outline of a face first appeared on the right side of the screen. On the left side was an icon (pictorial) menu showing mouth, eyes, nose, ears, and hair, from which children chose by pressing the space bar in a two-step procedure. Pressing the space bar caused one of the facial structures to light up. Subsequently pressing RETURN brought up a pictorial menu of styles for the chosen structure. For example, hair choices were long, short, curly, crew cut, male, female, and even bald. Most children, however, started building their face by pressing N for nose or E for eyes. Of the nose choices, a red, bulbous one was a particular favorite. Once they had selected the nose, the children pressed RETURN, and like magic the nose appeared on the head outline.

Choosing from pictorial menus caused problems for program operators at first, whether they were children or adults. Operators overshot their mark by pressing the space bar too fast. Then they had to go through the choices again until the letter of their choice lighted up. Naturally, children made a game of trying to get the cursor to stop on their chosen letter.

When the face was finally built, the children progressed to the second game, which proved to be the most fun: programming the features of the face to move. The operator programmed the face by typing in one-letter commands that stood for motions: W, wink; C, cry; T, tongue sticking out; F, frown; E, ear wiggling. We noted that children wanted to try out each movement separately rather than writing an integrated program, such as WWCTFEEE, which would make the face wink twice (WW), cry once (C), stick out its tongue once (T), frown once (F), and wiggle its ears three times (EEE). Instead, preschoolers wrote programs like WWWWWWWWW to make the eyes wink nine times when RETURN was pressed. Then they would go to the next motion and fill up the programming space with another single-letter command.

Because a sound accompanied each motion, the children were entranced by the face's performance. They played their programs again and again, never seeming to tire of the face's winks and wiggles. But, they did not make up stories. Perhaps because the program was so complicated or because the movements took place on a static object, the language stimulated by this program involved telling partners what the face was programmed to do or asking partners for instructions. Our children had not quite reached the meaning level with *Facemaker*. Had *Facemaker* been used at Halloween time, children could have pretended to be making Halloween masks.

In the meantime, children would say, "I want six winks," and fill in the program space with nine Ws, demonstrating once again that they had not truly learned one-to-one correspondence. To many youngsters six meant many, rather than the specific number 6.

One dialogue between two children who were taking turns with programming went like this:

> Boy: I'm gonna make him smile. Look, he's smiling!
>
> Girl: I'm gonna do it smiling.
>
> Boy: Let's see what happens.
>
> Girl: I'm gonna make his ears wiggle.
>
> Boy: I'm gonna do Q. Does that make him do anything?
>
> Girl: No.

Even though preschool children did not make up stories about the face during our six-week study, the fact remains that they learned to program a computer graphic to move by using simple command language. In addition, they had learned to use a multi-step program from which they could progress to more complex story-creating programs.

One problem confronting preschoolers using *Facemaker* is that their perceptual abilities have not developed sufficiently to allow them to recognize missing facial features. Some children put everything on the face except hair but cannot recognize what is missing until an adult points it out. Such omissions frequently show up in their drawings of people during this developmental stage. They often leave out noses or ears or hair. In fact, they seem programmed to perceive generalities at first, the refinement of detail recognition developing later.

## WHAT CHILDREN LEARNED FROM FACEMAKER

Although children did not make up their own stories using *Facemaker*, we were not by any means disappointed with their progress. It not only set the stage for more complicated programs, but it also continued the learning process started with earlier programs. The children's gains included:

1. Using a multi-stepped, complex program

2. Perfecting the eye-hand coordination necessary to stop the cursor on a particular letter

3. Perfecting the perceptual skills necessary to recognize what is missing on a face

4. Using simple commands to write a computer program

Once again, we noted that the program's success was due to the fact that children had direct control over it. The children seemed most attracted to programs over which they had direct control and could perform interesting actions by pressing particular keys.

## INTEGRATING FACEMAKER INTO THE CURRICULUM

*Facemaker* reminded us immediately of the commercial toy Mr. Potatohead; thus, we decided to use this toy to integrate making computer-programmed faces into the curriculum. The Potatohead family includes Mr. and Mrs. Potatohead and Baby and was an instant hit with the children. Plastic potato-shaped bodies come with hats, glasses, feet, arms, purses, eyes, noses, and other features and accessories that can be attached to make a complete potato person.

The toy was kept on the manipulative shelf where children could get to it during free play. Mr. Potatohead turned out to be as popular as the computer. Children made up stories about the potato people they created; they played with them like dolls, talking to them or about them and having them talk to each other. A favorite game was to dress Mr. and Mrs. Potatohead and Baby for a shopping excursion. The arms and legs of these dolls made them more mobile than the face on the computer and better able to move and talk, so far as the children were concerned.

Similar in nature is the dress-up corner. Be sure to provide it with hats, caps, visors, sunglasses, purses, wallets, belts, shopping bags, sneakers, sandals, wigs, and other interesting paraphernalia. The more exotic and different the props, the more exotic and different will be the children's pretending games. Dramatic play usually motivates the most language use by children.

Mask making is a fascinating activity that can grow out of children's use of *Facemaker*. Let children make their own masks from paper bags using paints, crayons, and collage materials. Children also love making clown faces on themselves using theatrical face paint and props, such as fake noses, mustaches, spectacles, and wigs. Many of these items can be found in stores at Halloween time.

Still another *Facemaker* activity is sound making. When the children are first introduced to the program, have them eliminate the sound that goes with each facial feature. Instead, let them make up their own sounds for winking, ear wiggling, crying, sticking out the tongue, and frowning. Have one child represent each sound. Let each child try to synchronize the sound with movement of the corresponding feature. If a child has programmed his or her face to wink eight times, then the child needs to make the sound eight times. Children may be slow at first and have more trouble stopping their sounds than starting them. Nevertheless, this can turn into an exciting learning activity if pursued for any length of time. Try different kinds of sounds on different days. Rhythm instruments also make excellent sounds. The children may want to tape record their sounds and save them for another day.

## PICTURE PROGRAMMING

Once children are familiar with programs as complex as *Facemaker* and have learned to control graphic movement with simple commands, they will be able to operate with ease a story program such as *Picture Programming*. With this program, children choose the actors and what they want them to do in the story. There are five troupes of twelve actors each from which children can select their characters. For instance, the gentle troupe includes:

| | |
|---|---|
| 1 = Bear | 7 = Cat |
| 2 = Turtle | 8 = Bird |
| 3 = Snake | 9 = Horse |
| 4 = Pig | 0 = Flower |
| 5 = Dog | : = Stump |
| 6 = Lamb | - = Tree |

The other four troupes are adventure, aqua, circus, and princess. Children choose their characters by pressing corresponding number keys. For movement, a set of action icons appears from which the operator selects according to symbol. For instance:

1 = Select a new actor

2 = Play music

3 = Recolor the actor

4 = Turn actor upside down

5 = Turn actor completely around

6 = Move left

7 = Move right

8 = Move up

9 = Move down

% = Go to lower left corner

Once children have constructed a movie, as the program is called, they can make up a story about the characters and their actions. Young children tend to make up stories after they have created their movie or as they are doing it, rather than making up the story first and then programming the actors. The teacher can record their stories on tape or on an experience chart to be played or read when the computer program is run.

## ACTIVITIES TO USE WITH COMPUTER STORY PROGRAMS

Several acvities lend themselves to use with story programs. In particular, field trips and fanciful storybooks should help children to explore the reaches of their imaginations.

### Make Up Stories

Teachers can motivate children to make up stories about computer graphics by encouraging them to make up and tell stories about other preschool activities. During field trips, the teacher should write down in story form what children have to say about the trip. Such can be accomplished using newsprint, a felt-tipped marker, and an easel (an experience chart) with each member of the group contributing to the story. Or, the teacher might ask a small group or individual to tell their own stories about the trip. The story can be recorded in a blank book, a scrapbook illustrated with photos of the trip, or on cassette tape.

You don't know where to go on a field trip? A book such as Rhoda Redleaf's *Open the Door Let's Explore: Neighborhood Field Trips for Young Children* (St. Paul, Minn.: Toys 'n' Things Press, 1983) presents ideas for simple trips from "tree walks, truck walks, and windy day walks" to the more traditional grocery stores and hospitals. The book includes many follow-up activities from games and dramatic play to songs and finger plays.

If children show interest in having their trip stories written or tape recorded and then read or played back, they may want to continue making up stories about their trip on other days. Can they tell the story about the trip from the point of view of a pretend kitten or puppy that went along? If they visit a farm, can they tell the story of the trip from the point of view of a cow or sheep? If they visit a fire station, can they make up a story about the visit from the point of view of a fire engine? Children love to hear stories about personified animals and objects, especially vehicles. Making up stories expands their imaginations. Personal experiences, such as field trips, create images that can be tapped for whimsical stories.

### Read Stories Featuring Imagination

Many children's books feature talking animals, imaginary creatures, or fanciful situations. Read some of these stories to children to motivate them to make up similar stories of their own. When you have finished the story, ask the children what they would have done in the same situation. You may want to record their replies. Don Freeman's *The Paper Party* (New York: Penguin Books, 1977) shows a little boy who climbs into his television set to attend a papier-mâche party given by the characters of the TV program he is watching.

John Burningham's *Time to Get out of the Bath, Shirley* (New York: Thomas Y. Crowell, 1978) illustrates the wildly imaginative adventures of Shirley, who floats through the drain of the bathtub into a magic land of knights and kings (on the right-hand pages of the book). On the left-hand pages, her mother stands in the bathroom and, without looking at Shirley, talks matter-of-factly about getting out of the bathtub, folds the towel, and picks up Shirley's clothes.

Wordless picture books are also excellent for motivating children to make up stories. Mercer Mayer's *The Great Cat Chase* (New York: Four Winds Press, 1974) is a small format book showing children wearing dress-up clothes with their cat in a baby buggy. The cat rejects its role and runs away in a topsy-turvy chase that everyone loses until they change the play to nurse and doctor. Several other wordless books by Mayer can be used in the same way.

## OBSERVING CHILDREN USING STORY PROGRAMS

Teachers concerned with children's language development should find out what children talk about as they use programs. Do they play with words and sounds? Do they make up words or talk about them? Do they make up stories or pretend about the graphics on the screen? Do they mostly converse with a partner about other things? To find out, teachers can observe the computer operators unobtrusively and record their language on a running record.

Some teachers want a more focused account of each child's language production with directions on what to look for. For them a language checklist is useful (table 4).

As a backup to a checklist or running record, you may want to tape record children's conversations at the computer. Place a small cassette recorder on the table next to the keyboard and turn it on when children use the machine. Tapes provide valuable information about language development if you use them as soon as possible after they have been recorded. Plan to transcribe the tapes on the same day they are recorded. Otherwise, they may lose much of their meaning and value. We tend to forget what we were looking for, who did the talking, and details that would clarify taped dialogues. Transferring taped speech to an individual checklist gives the teacher an easy-to-use record of language usage and a means to analyze language development.

**TABLE 4.**   Computer language checklist

| Name | Age |
|---|---|
| Name of Partner | Age |
| Date | Time on Computer |
| Title of Program | |

|  | Type of Language Used | Record of Dialogue |
|---|---|---|
| _____ | Turn-taking conversation | |
| _____ | Self-talk | |
| _____ | Question asking, answering | |
| _____ | Direction giving | |
| _____ | Comments about program | |
| _____ | Comments about actions to be taken | |
| _____ | Critiquing partner's actions | |
| _____ | Exclamations | |
| _____ | Word or sound play | |
| _____ | Story creation or pretending | |

Playing back recorded tapes also helps the teacher determine which of the computer programs is the best chatterbox, that is, the best stimulator of children's language. Such programs should then be made available to children as often as possible.

# REFERENCES

Beaty, Janice J. *Observing Development of the Young Child.* Columbus, Ohio: Merrill Publishing Co., 1986.

Beaty, Janice J. and W. Hugh Tucker. *Becoming Partners with a Computer: Preschoolers Learn How.* 1985. Elmira, N.Y.: 3-to-5. P.O. Box 3213, 14905. Videotape.

Beaty, Janice J., and W. Hugh Tucker. *Computer in the Preschool: An Integrated Activity.* 1985. Elmira, N.Y.: 3-to-5. P.O. Box 3213, 14905. Slides and Tape.

Berk, Laura E. "Why Children Talk to Themselves." *Young Children* 40, no. 5 (July 1985): 46–52.

**Chukovsky, Kornei.** *From Two to Five.* Berkeley: University of California Press, 1968.

**Cron, Mary.** "Spinnaker's Learning Games: Celebrating Halloween in the Computer Age." *Popular Computing,* (August 1983): 196-200.

**Glazer, Joan I.** *Literature for Young Children.* 2d ed. Columbus, Ohio: Merrill Publishing Co., 1986.

**Holzman, Matilda.** *The Language of Children.* Englewood Cliffs, N.J.: Prentice-Hall, 1983.

**Murphy, Brian J.** "Educational Programs for the Very Young." *Creative Computing,* (October 1983): 107-118.

**Schwartz, Judith I.** "Children's Experiments with Language." *Young Children* 36, no. 5 (July 1981): 16-26.

**Wood, Barbara S.** *Children and Communication: Verbal and Nonverbal Development.* Englewood Cliffs, N.J.: Prentice-Hall, 1981.

## SOFTWARE

*Alf in the Color Caves*
>     Spinnaker Software Corp.
>     One Kendall Square
>     Cambridge, Mass. 02139

Atari 400, 800, all XLs; Commodore 64; ROM cartridge.

With this program children learn to manuever Alf through a maze. They can make up a story as they go along. (Grades preschool–1)

*Dragon's Keep*
>     Sierra On-Line, Inc.
>     P.O. Box 485
>     Coarsegold, Calif. 93614

Apple II family, high resolution graphics, 1983

A game in which the operator tries to rescue an animal from a room where a dragon may appear. Several screens of written directions, including three statements of possibilities at bottom of each picture from which the child must choose. Adult help is necessary for preliterate children at first. Good for motivating children to make up stories once they have mastered the mechanics.

*Early Games for Young Children: Draw*
>     Springboard Software, Inc.
>     7807 Creekridge Circle
>     Minneapolis, Minn. 55435

Apple II family, 48K; disk drive; IBM PC; Commodore 64; VIC–20; TRS–80 Model I, III; Atari; 1984

Discussed in this chapter and in chapter 7. (Grades preschool–1)

*Facemaker*

Spinnaker Software Corp.
215 First St.
Cambridge, Mass. 02142

Apple II+, IIe; Atari 400, 800, 1200; Commodore 64; IBM PC
Discussed in this chapter. (Grades preschool and up)

*Grandma's House*

Spinnaker Software Corp.
215 First St.
Cambridge, Mass. 02142

Apple II family, 48K, disk drive, joystick; Atari 400, 800, all XLs; Commodore 64
Children need a joystick to operate this program. They choose actors from
among 30 characters. Then their actor can go into a variety of scenes and
choose items to be brought back to Grandma's House and placed in the
various rooms. Once children have mastered the program, they can make up
stories about the actors and actions. (Grades preschool–3)

*Imagination: Picture Programming*

Wiley Professional Software
John Wiley & Sons
605 Third Ave.
New York, N.Y. 10158

Apple II family, 64K, disk drive
Discussed in this chapter. (Grades K–6)

*Jeepers Creatures*

Kangaroo, Inc.
110 S. Michigan
Chicago, Ill. 60605

Apple II family, disk drive; Atari
Discussed in this chapter and chapter 3.

*Kermit's Electronic Story Maker*

Simon and Schuster
1230 Avenue of the Americas
New York, N.Y. 10020

Apple II family, uses keys or joystick
Operator can flip through Muppet pictures and write picture stories with them.
(Grades K–3)

*Kids at Work*

Scholastic, Inc.
730 Broadway
New York, N.Y. 10003

Apple II family
A program like *Grandma's House* without a joystick. Keys move people figures
around to pick up items from city or country scenes and move them into
buildings. Children can make up stories about the buildings they are filling up.
(Grades K and up)

*Mask Parade*
> Springboard Software, Inc.
> 7807 Creekridge Circle
> Minneapolis, Minn. 55435

Apple II family, low-resolution graphics, 1984
Keys or joystick help children select and create masks, badges, feet, jewelry, and glasses, which can then be printed, cut out, colored, and worn by the children in their dramatic play—an intriguing idea! Operator does not have as much control over building his creation as in *Facemaker*.

*Mr. and Mrs. Potatohead*
> Random House
> 201 E. 50th St.
> New York, N.Y. 10022

Apple II family, high-resolution graphics
Children can add parts to a potato and then program it to move as with *Facemaker*. This program, however, has high-resolution graphics with several more realistic backgrounds. Lends itself to making up stories.

*My Book*
> Boston Educational Computing, Inc.
> 78 Dartmouth St.
> Boston, Mass. 02116

Commodore 64, requires joystick, 64K, 1984
Children can choose different people and settings and arrange them any way they want to make up their own stories.

*Nursery Time*
> Merry Bee Communications
> 815 Crest Drive-Papillion
> Omaha, Nebr. 68046

Apple, DOS 3.3, 48K, disk drive
This program is an electronic book with music, color, action, a hidden letter challenge and a prompt for the user's own storytelling. (Grades preschool–2)

*Picture Perfect*
> Mindplay/Methods and Solutions, Inc.
> 300 Unicorn Park Dr.
> Woburn, Mass. 01801

Apple II Series, DOS 3.3, 48K, disk
Children can choose different pictures, lines, shapes, and colors and place them on a computer "drawing pad." Then stories can be made up about them. (Grades preschool and up)

*Play House*
> Harper and Row Publishers
> Orders to: Keystone Industrial Park
> Scranton, Pa. 18512

Apple II family; Commodore 64, color monitor

Similar to *Grandma's House*. In this program, the operator goes into the house on the computer screen, looks around, chooses and places family members and furniture. Then he or she can make up a story about the family.

**Sammy the Sea Serpent**

        Program Design, Inc.

        11 Idar Court

        Greenwich, Conn. 06830

Atari, disk, cassette tape, joystick

Children listen to a story of Sammy's adventures on a computer-controlled cassette tape player. The computer operators are then asked to help Sammy move by using a joystick to help him overcome obstacles and continue on his adventures until he arrives home.

**The Three Bears**

        Millennium Group, Inc.

        24 E. 22nd St.

        New York, N.Y. 10010

Apple II family, DOS 3.3, 48K, disk drive

Children direct the actions in this classic fairy tale.


## LEARNING ACTIVITIES

1.  Observe and record the language of several of your children at the computer by using the Computer Language Checklist (table 4). What is the most prevalent type of language that you hear?

2.  Use a cassette recorder to record your children's language as they work at the computer. What types of language do you find on the tape when you listen to it afterwards? How does this compare with the language you recorded in activity 1?

3.  Use a drawing program with your children. Record any of the stories they make up about their pictures. How can you support the creation of the same kinds of stories in other classroom activities? Try your idea and see what happens.

4.  Take your children on a field trip and then provide them with props to recreate their trip in the classroom. Record any stories or pretend play they tell or do.

5.  Use wordless picture books with individuals or small groups. Record the stories children make up on paper or tape. Have these stories available for children to listen to later.

# Choosing Software for the Preliterate Child

N ew software for personal computers is being developed every day. Someone someplace is working on virtually every conceivable computer application. In this rapidly changing environment how does the concerned preschool professional choose the best software for early child development?

One of the best ways we have found is to study carefully what is available and then try out programs that seem to fit your personal philosophy of how young children learn. The basic philosophy of this book is that young children are self-taught through play. A large number of preschool programs are based on this philosophy and, therefore, have set up their classrooms for children to learn independently. If this is your philosophy, then you should look for computer software that supports choice and independence as learning goals.

A contrasting philosophy is that good education consists of learning through instruction and reinforcement of goals by reward. If this is your philosophy, then you should look for computer programs that control children's responses and feature strong positive reinforcements.

The first philosophy reflects a developmental approach to learning theory; the second, a behavioristic approach. Preschool programs can be found that reflect both approaches to learning. Seymour Papert contrasts these two approaches by asking whether it is the role of the child to program the computer or the role of the computer to program the child (Papert 1980, 5).

Many first-generation educational computer programs, such as *Juggle's Rainbow*, reflect the behavioristic approach. The child is presented with a problem, such as to pick the object on the right. When the correct answer is given, the child is rewarded with positive reinforcement, such as an animated picture. There are many programs on the market that reflect this philosophy. The curricular goals are clearly stated for such software. In its purest form, this type of programming does not reinforce "off task" (original) behavior. Off-task behavior is either ignored or "rewarded" with a negative reinforcer, such as a frowning face or harsh sound.

The developmental approach to writing software, on the other hand, provides the child with maximum control over the program and allows the imagination to create stories and games using the computer as a play medium. Most of the drawing, painting, and chatterbox programs described in this book represent this approach to preschool learning. Some programs, such as *Learning with Leeper*, consciously combine both approaches while others, such as the *Stickybear* series, represent a behavioristic approach to programming but have enough creative latitude in the execution of the program to allow children to develop alternative ways of using it. Both programming philosophies have legitimate roles in the preschool curriculum, but the balance and sequencing of the programs should reflect the overall philosophy of the preschool.

## HOW TO FIND NEW PROGRAMS

Finding new programs can be made easier with a systematic approach to the task. There is a wealth of information available in magazines, books, catalogs, and software reviews, each of which are discussed below.

### Magazines

The best way to discover new programs for the preschool child is to read the trade journals. This includes both early childhood professional journals, such as *Childhood Education* and *Young Children*, as well as computer magazines. If you are shopping for a computer, it is useful to read the reviews of early childhood software in computer magazines designed for the casual user, such as *Compute!* and *Personal Computing*. These magazines along with the trade newspaper *InfoWorld* are useful for entering the personal computer culture.

If you are working with a specific computer, there are many magazines that specialize in writing for a specific brand. Most of these magazines concentrate on reviews of software and hardware for that brand of computer. Examples of computer-specific magazines are *InCider* for the Apple II and Macintosh, *Antic: The Atari Resource* for Atari computers, *Commodore: The Microcomputer Magazine* for computers made by Commodore, and *PC World* for IBM PCs.

Many computer magazines review educational and home software. One of the best times to look for reviews of early childhood software is in the fall. September issues usually carry articles and reviews of educational software, while the December and January issues concentrate on home software. The early childhood market is generally considered to be a home rather than an educational market.

You might also want to look at computer magazines and journals designed specifically for educators. Examples of this type of magazine are *Enter* from Children's Television Workshop, *Electronic Learning* from Scholastic, Inc., and the *Computing Teacher* published by the International Council for Computers in Education.

## Books, Clearinghouse Publications, Catalogs

Other sources of reviews and information about preschool programs are books such as *Only the Best: The Discriminating Software Guide for Preschool–Grade 12* and the *Parent-Teacher's Microcomputing Sourcebook For Children, 1985*. Software reviews are also published by media clearinghouses, such as the California Library Media Consortium. A partial list of magazines, books, and catalogs can be found at the end of this chapter. Perhaps the most valuable information can be gleaned by talking to individuals who use computers in an early childhood setting, including parents with young children who use a home computer. In the end, there is no substitute for directly observing children using a personal computer.

## REVIEWING REVIEWS

A good review should give an accurate description of the program so that the reader can determine whether it fits his or her needs and desires. Look at any illustrations of the actual screen to determine the quality of the graphics. Are the graphics high-resolution, resulting in more sophisticated, fully colored screens? Or are they low-resolution, the earlier, simpler screens with a lot of black background? Are the graphics animated or still? Animation holds young children's interest more than still pictures.

Ask yourself the following questions about the review. Does the reviewer have a bias? Does this bias affect the objectivity of the review? Does the reviewer really understand preschool children, or is his or her orientation based on experience with older children? Has the reviewer actually seen preschool children use the program?

To illustrate, let's consider a review of *Stickybear ABC* that appeared in a professional journal. The reviewer critiqued the program as if it were an alphabet book, rather than an interactive computer program. The reviewer discussed the poor choice of words representing specific letters because they contained initial blends (for example, *gr* in *grass*.) The reviewer also cited research indicating that mechanical ABC programs repressed conversation between parent and child. The reviewer completely ignored how children really use the program in a preschool setting, how much conversation is generated, and how children acquire new letters and new vocabulary.

Popular magazines, such as *Commodore: The Microcomputer Magazine,* have more reviews of early childhood computer programs based on direct observation than do professional journals. The first lesson learned in the Elmira Project was that adult assumptions (our own!) about how children will use a program are rarely sustained when the children are observed actually using the program.

## REVIEWING SOFTWARE FOR PURCHASE

The best way to evaluate software is your own observation of the program on a computer. If possible, observe one or two children using the program. The child should be of the same age and computer experience as the children who will be using the software in the preschool program. Observe the child's ability to concentrate on the program. Does the program hold the child's interest? Is the program age-appropriate? Many programs list unrealistic age levels. If the prescribed age level is too low, the child will quickly become bored with the program; if it is too high, the child may become frustrated and walk away.

There are also some ethical issues that should be considered when evaluating software. Does the software represent values that are important for preschool children to develop? For instance, one issue in evaluating game programs is that of violence. Many game programs involve the destruction of objects on the screen and thus reinforce the notion that violence solves problems. These programs may also display a disastrous consequence (such as being killed or blown up) if a mistake is made. Violent programs are of questionable ethical value in the education of young children. On the other hand, programs that promote cooperation and building objects on the screen should be encouraged.

## EXTENT OF ADULT ASSISTANCE

How much adult supervision or instruction is required before the child can use the program independently? Programs that require a high level of adult supervision fall into two categories. The first category includes programs for young children that assume literacy. Many programs listed as age-appropriate for preschool children either assume that children can read by the time they are four or that the child will sit on an adult lap while the adult reads the "electronic book" on the screen. A number of programs based on nursery rhymes fit into this category. These programs should be rejected out of hand by the early childhood educator as misuse of the medium. Books are more appropriate and cheaper than such computer programs.

The second type of software requiring adult help includes programs that incorporate various commands. Examples are the *Imagination* series, *Delta Drawing*, and *Facemaker*. These programs are more difficult to evaluate because they may be within the capability of an experienced user but are very frustrating to the novice. After an initial introduction by an adult, young children can learn to operate these programs on their own. However, teachers need to be aware that such programs work more successfully when introduced later in the year after children have become familiar with the keyboard. A rule of thumb used by some teachers to evaluate software is that programs labeled 4–7 years generally require some reading, while those labeled 3–7 years do not.

Teachers also need to look for visual cues in such programs that help the child remember the commands. Does the program contain a pictorial menu? Does the child understand what action each symbol represents? Pictorial reminders of commands not only help nonreaders use the computer independently, they are also faster and more convenient for the person who can read. Children need to use computer programs on their own after an initial introduction. If the program requires adult supervision every time it is used, it is not age-appropriate.

## EXTENT OF THE CHILD'S CONTROL

Children need to control actively what the program does. Many programs take important features out of the child's control. A program may generate a scene or a graphic in a random manner when a child presses a key. This makes it difficult for the child to relocate favorite parts of the program. When children invent a game using a particular graphic, they need to find it easily by means of their own control over the program.

It is wise to ask whether the program rewards all correct actions by the child. This principle is difficult to state briefly but easy to illustrate. An ABC program should allow the preschool child to explore all of the letter keys at one time. *Charley Brown's ABC* for the Apple II computer has outstanding graphics and animation but suffers from one fatal flaw: the first half of the alphabet is on one side of the disk and the second half is on the other side. Therefore, only one half of the alphabet is available to the child at any one time. Fifty percent of the time the child receives no reward for pressing a letter key. Children should not be expected to go through half of the alphabet and then turn over the disk to go through the rest. This would be an outstanding program if it were complete on one side of the disk, but in its present form for the Apple II, it is unacceptable.

## Reinforcers

A program may use a slide show (an automatic sequence of pictures) or some other passive device to reward the user for proper actions. Some programmers seem to feel that the way to reward children or draw them into the program is to put on a show. Examples of this philosophy can be found in many programs. *Jeepers Creatures* has a slide show of ten animals in its zoo (see chapter 3). While the zoo is being presented, the computer is controlled by the program, not the child. Some children enjoy this show, but most become bored and restless because they want to control the computer, rather than watch it. In like manner, *Dinosaurs* rewards the child with a dinosaur parade after correct completion of a matching test. The first time it appears, the dinosaur parade is rather appealing, but the enjoyment fades with repetition. In reality, the best positive reinforcer for children doing a program task correctly is success itself.

The best negative reinforcement for incorrect actions is for the program to ignore them. Many programs do not respond when a child makes a mistake. To find out how a program treats mistakes, make one deliberately and see what happens. Is there a loud, unpleasant sound or frowning face? How do you feel about that? Listen to your own emotions. If the program upsets you, it will probably upset a preschool child. Avoid programs that use highly aversive responses to wrong actions. Children may either find such negative reinforcement so embarrassing that they leave the computer, or so funny that they make a game of it. Thus, the program ends up reinforcing incorrect responses. Bright children often make mistakes deliberately to see what will happen.

## Keyboard Considerations

What happens if the child uses a key that is not required by the program? A good preschool computer program should disable all keys not used by the program. Some programs provide a short, abrasive sound when a wrong key is pushed, while others ignore the mistake and do nothing. If you use a Commodore, the program should control the keyboard functions and disable the key with the Commodore logo and the shift/lock key. The principle is that only useful keys be active.

Is it possible for the user to stop the program execution in the middle of the task? It should be. There should be some way to leave the program gracefully at any time if the user becomes bored and wants to turn it over to another child. The escape key is often used to exit a program and return the user to the beginning of the program.

*Be sure to obtain copies of programs.*

## Keyboard versus External Devices

Is the software controlled by the keyboard or does it require an external device, such as a joystick, mouse, touch pad, or touch screen? Contrary to adult wisdom, the easiest control device for young children is the keyboard. If every key does something, children as young as two can enjoy a keyboard-controlled program. Children like using the keyboard. It is an adult activity that they can do. Early childhood researchers have found that "Children as young as 3 are quite able to use a standard keyboard. Indeed, given that a 6-month-old infant can pick up a raisin, it is surprising that we ever doubted that preschoolers could cope with the keyboard." The same researchers go on to note that adult astonishment over little children operating a computer keyboard "reveals more about adult mystification and ignorance of the microcomputer than it does about the apparent precocity of preschoolers using microcomputers" (Borgh and Dickson 1986, 39).

The primary consideration with respect to having keyboard control is the program's complexity, not the child's ability to master a particular external device. During an activity with *MacPaint* on the Apple Macintosh, three- and four-year-old children were as interested in typing random letters on the screen as they were in drawing pictures with a mouse.

The keyboard also offers the advantage of being easy to share. It does not involve giving up possession of a hand-held instrument. Children should be able to use the keyboard without the use of templates (fiber or metal masks placed over unused keys), stickers, or other keyboard aids. If a normal child needs such devices to find proper keys, then either the child is not developmentally ready for the program, or the program is poorly conceived.

If the program uses an external device, such as a joystick or a mouse, the child should be able to give commands to the program with a minimum of frustration. The program should guard against the tendency of joysticks to relay commands to the computer faster than the program can respond. The results can be frustrating. All but the most expensive joysticks require very fine motor control for precise operation.

We were very excited about the possibilities for imaginative play with *Grandma's House*. This program provides a dollhouse with side trips to the park, the city, and the jungle, using only a joystick. However, in field testing, children were frustrated by the lack of precise control with the joystick, which tended to allow scene changes before the children were ready. The program was abandoned before mastery was reached. *Learning with Leeper,* on the other hand, restricts movement of the cursor and requires a button on the joystick to be pushed to change scenes.

As with software, the best test of an external device is to observe a child using it. Perhaps the best solution to the keyboard versus external device issue is software that gives the user a choice between the two.

## SOFTWARE CHECKLIST

A software checklist can help when reviewing computer software for possible purchase (table 5). Each of the issues for consideration is listed as a separate item. As you might expect, not every item can be checked for every piece of software. It is necessary to prioritize according to the philosophy and needs of your preschool program. If you plan to review the software at

**TABLE 5.** Software checklist

| Program Under Consideration |
| --- |
| _____ Represents appropriate learning goals |
| _____ Can be used by child without reading skills |
| _____ Holds child's interest |
| _____ Represents acceptable ethical values |
| _____ Does not require extensive adult assistance |
| _____ Uses high-resolution graphics |
| _____ Has animated graphics |
| _____ Has graphics controlled by child (not random) |
| _____ Uses success as positive reinforcement for task completion |
| _____ Has no attention-getting negative reinforcers |
| _____ Allows only program keys to be active |
| _____ Allows child to exit program any time with escape key |
| _____ Uses keyboard and/or external control |
| _____ Has provision for copies or replacement disks |

a dealer's store, take a young child along to help you try it out. If you are a preschool teacher or director, ask your local school district or nearby college whether they own any of the programs you have read about in the reviews. Or send home a request in your newsletter for parents who might own a particular program to let you try it out.

## COPIES AND REPLACEMENT DISKS

Computer software is highly reliable but, as with any manufactured product, it is wise to make plans for those times when things go wrong. Disks and tapes sometimes wear out or become damaged. Reasonable precautions can prevent many problems.

      If the disk or tape can be copied, you should make a copy of the original program and use the copy in the classroom. The original should be put in a safe place and only be used to make more copies. A copy program is normally found on the system's utility disk that comes with the computer. One of the first tasks of a new computer owner should be to learn to use this program and copy the system's utility disk itself.

      Copyright law allows the user to make one copy strictly for archival purposes. It is illegal to sell or give copies of the program to other preschools or individuals. It is also a violation to make multiple copies and use them on other computers within a single organization.

The best precaution against failure of copy-protected software is to obtain copies. Many software producers will supply a copy for a nominal fee and proof of purchase. They often do not advertise this service. When you buy the program, you should register your software and ask the company for its policy for supplying replacement disks and/or backups. If the documentation that comes with the program gives the purchase price of a replacement disk, you should order it as part of the registration process. An extra copy of the program can prevent headaches in the long run.

## PROTECTING SOFTWARE

There are several ways to protect your software. On standard $5\frac{1}{4}$-inch disks there may be a square notch cut into the right side of the disk. This is called a write protect notch. If it is not there or if it is covered with a piece of tape (such as the small silver or black strips of tape supplied with blank disks), the computer cannot write to the disk. You should cover this notch with a strip of tape to avoid accidental damage or erasure.

Another precaution is to store disks in a cool, dry place away from sunlight. Extremes in temperature or humidity damage disks. You should always keep the disk in its original jacket to protect it from dust and mishandling when it is not in use. You should also keep disks away from magnets. Sources of magnets in a preschool are magnetic toys, operational telephones, objects with bells and buzzers, and the backs of television sets and computer monitors.

## PURCHASING SOFTWARE

Preschools operate on tight budgets. The cost of buying a computer and providing necessary software is a matter of real concern. The average retail cost for preschool software is in the range of twenty-five to forty dollars per disk. Prices range from free for software in the public domain (usually not of commercial quality) to hundreds of dollars for a complete set of commercial-quality disks.

What constitutes a reasonable budget for a preschool software purchase? The first question in making this decision is How many software programs does the preschool need? The first year of use should represent the largest budgetary commitment. Selection involves a careful look at how the programs will be sequenced.

For the first year, you might consider trying a program-of-the-month plan with a different program (or game from a program) each month. Some preschool disks, such as *Learning with Leeper,* have more than one game on the disk. With multiple-game disks, you can concentrate at first on one game at a time, rather than give unlimited choices to the children. Thus, one disk can last for more than one month. When the class has become familiar with all of the games on the disk, allow them to choose freely.

Restrict free time with the computer to programs children already know. Although they may be quite capable of using all of the new programs, you may be faced with the "birthday party phenomenon," a situation in which children are attracted to the novelty of new toys but fail to explore the possibilities inherent in each one. Children need time to explore all aspects of a program and should reach a level of mastery before moving on to a new one.

The preschool dollar can be stretched by pulling programs out of circulation and then reintroducing them at a later date. With proper sequencing, a preschool should be able to build a good software collection by purchasing five to ten programs a year. This constitutes a budget commitment of $200 to $500 a year at today's prices. With careful purchases, a preschool can have an outstanding software library by the end of the second year.

## SEQUENCING SOFTWARE

Sequencing is important in any skill-based curriculum. Preschool children go through a chronological process of learning that includes inducing rules, testing the rules, making generalizations, testing the generalizations, unlearning overgeneralizations, making new rules, and testing the new rules. A well-planned curriculum facilitates this process by building on the foundation of old skills and generalizations. The preschool professional needs to be concerned about sequencing because it determines the effectiveness of a program.

Children learn best at the preschool age by pursuing fun activities. Computer software that has been selected because it meets such needs must be carefully integrated into the curriculum. Computer activities also must be sequenced from easy to difficult so that each experience with the computer is under the child's control and is a successful, playful experience. The first program should use most of the keyboard and allow a great degree of autonomy. Such features encourage exploration and familiarity with the machine. They develop self-confidence and mastery, which then provide an emotional foundation for the more difficult tasks to come.

The first encounters with the keyboard should be exploratory. The child should begin to recognize specific keys and deduce cause-and-effect relationships that exist between pressing a specific key and having something enjoyable happen on the screen. Such experiences provide a foundation for advancing to programs that require a smaller portion of the keyboard, such as cursor control or number keys. The child learns the new program by testing it, unlearning rules generated from the previous program, and developing a new set of rules. Eventually, the foundation is laid for advancing to more complicated, command-controlled software.

Using a program can extend over an entire year as children move through the stages of manipulation, mastery, and meaning. When the class becomes bored with a program, set it aside and reintroduce it later in the year. After the children become thoroughly comfortable with keyboard control, you might want to introduce externally-controlled programs, such as *Learning with Leeper* or the *Stickybear* series, to work on fine-motor control.

The sequence should move from programs that use most of the keyboard to programs that use part of the keyboard to programs that use selected keys. Programs that use joysticks or keyboard commands should be introduced late in the sequence. Complex programs using a series of commands should be allotted more time than relatively simple programs.

## SEQUENCE TABLE

Software programs can be sequenced into a nine-month preschool program according to computer literacy objectives (table 6). In addition to the skills and learning objectives discussed in the preceding chapters, children can achieve computer literacy in a natural, step-by-step manner. Other computer programs carefully selected according to your own goals and objectives can serve the same purpose.

## SOFTWARE IN A CRYSTAL BALL

New, exciting, and easier-to-use preschool programs will be emerging on a regular basis. The need for preschool software that challenges the imagination of the young child will never be totally satisfied. The major problem with software development is the tendency to imitate existing software rather than forge new directions.

There is a need for more adventure games for preliterate children. Adventure games are best-sellers for literate children and adults, but virtually all of the adventure games on the market today require literacy. Even *Gertrude's Secrets,* a problem-solving game for children five through eight, requires literacy to read the directions. A preschool adventure game should use graphics and involve simple decisions, rather than difficult puzzles. It should encourage children to develop their own stories to explain the actions on the screen and encourage cooperation between partners. In the future, such a program might use voice commands to give directions or clues. It should involve exciting adventures, not violence.

A real-life simulation is a form of adventure game that is particularly worthwhile. An interactive story with animation, for example, could be based on cooking a meal, something truly fascinating to the three to five year old. Such a game could include a trip to the grocery store to buy the ingredients, cooking the meal, setting the table, eating the meal, and cleaning up afterward. The game could use a combination of voice output and graphics. Each

**TABLE 6.** Sequence for using computer software

| | Example Programs | Computer Literacy Objectives | Supportive Activities |
|---|---|---|---|
| Month 1 | Jeepers Creatures or Kiri's Hodge Podge | To insert disk, turn on monitor and computer To press any key and bring up graphic | Field trip to zoo or farm Animal puzzles Books: A Funny Fish Story or Fish Is Fish |
| Month 2 | Stickybear ABC or Kiri's Hodge Podge | To press certain letter key and bring up letter graphic To learn location of certain letter keys | Magnetic letters Alphabet soup Alphabet books |
| Month 3 | Stickybear Numbers | To learn location of number keys To press number keys and cause that number of objects to appear To press space bar to add or subtract objects | Dominoes, counting games, toy cash register, magnetic numbers Counting books |
| Month 4 | Stickybear Opposites | To learn location and use of cursor control keys | Opposite games and songs Opposite books |
| Month 5 | Dinosaurs or Stickybear Shapes | To choose from menu with cursor control keys and space bar (Shapes) or RETURN key (Dinosaurs) To choose correct shape or dinosaur with cursor control keys and space bar or RETURN | Matching games, lotto, shape games Make dinosaur from clay Dinosaur and shape books |

**TABLE 6.** Sequence for using computer software, *continued*

|  | *Example Programs* | *Computer Literacy Objectives* | *Supportive Activities* |
|---|---|---|---|
| Month 6 | *Early Games: Draw* or other draw programs | To choose *Draw* from moving menu with RETURN key To draw with cursor and keys in different sections of board To change colors with space bar To erase with cursor or ESCAPE key | Etch-a-Sketch Crayons and markers on paper Colored chalk on board |
| Month 7 | *Learning with Leeper* or other paint programs | To choose from menu with joystick To move paint cursor with joystick To change color with joystick | Easel painting or table painting with brush and same colors as computer program Finger painting with same colors |
| Month 8 | *Facemaker* | To set up program by answering Y (yes) or N (no) to questions To choose games and features with number and letter keys To write simple action program with letter keys | Mr. Potato Head toy Make paper bag masks Dramatic play with face makeup, false noses, mustaches, and spectacles |
| Month 9 | *Picture Programming* | To choose characters for story with number keys To choose actions for story with number keys To write simple action program with number keys | Make up stories from wordless picture books Make up stories about Stickybear or Mr. Potato Head Tape record story Write stories on experience chart |

step in the process should allow decisions, such as what to buy, how to cook it, who should sit at the table, who should wash dishes, who should take out the garbage. Another simulation might be a visit to a farm or ranch.

The third generation of home computers, the Commodore Amiga, the Apple Macintosh, and the Atari 520ST, offer exciting opportunities for developing adventure and simulation games for preschool children. Existing programs such as *Grandma's House, Sammy the Sea Serpent,* and *Ranch* offer first-generation examples of this type of preschool program.

## MUSIC PROGRAMS

Music for preschool children represents another area in need of creative exploration. Most existing programs are based on teaching traditional musical notation. Preschool children need programs that encourage exploring and playing with sound and rhythm. Such a program might involve sounds linked to computer drawing and painting.

Many programs use sounds or music as reinforcers. Children enjoy interesting sounds. Music is often used to reinforce an action. For example, the ABC programs associate music with letters. The letter *S* has a sailboat graphic, and the child hears a nautical tune. Observers note that preschool children often "dance" in their chairs during these tunes. It is obvious that they enjoy music tremendously. The preschooler should be able to control the length of the tune by continuing that part of the program for as long as he or she wants. Programs that have a preset length of time for the tune and accompanying graphics are less satisfactory.

There are a few programs on the market for preschool children that allow them to play with sounds just as drawing and painting programs allow them to play with graphics. One such program is *Kiri's Hodge Podge.* This program assigns each of the number keys to a note on the musical scale. Thus, a child can play a note by pressing a number key. Every key plays a different note. Although the graphics in *Kiri's Hodge Podge* are not very sophisticated, the use of sound is excellent.

*Early Games for Young Children: Music* and the music disk in the *Imagination* series are designed specifically for teaching musical notation. *Early Games for Young Children: Music* contains a number of games drawn from a moving menu that requires reading skills. Each picture on the moving menu represents a group of functions, such as the position of notes on a keyboard, treble clef, and bass clef. The options within each function are written at the bottom of the screen. Most of the exercises consist of matching the note that is missing from the musical staff on the screen with its associated letter on the computer keyboard. For instance, a question mark in the A note position means the child must push the letter A to continue. Such exercises are of questionable value for the preschool child.

There is one feature of *Early Games for Young Children: Music* that is fun for preschoolers: the set of number keys can be used as a musical keyboard. Each key plays a note and creates part of a low-resolution design.

This is the only feature that allows the child to control and play with the program: a major criterion for selecting preschool software. The purpose of *Early Games for Young Children: Music* is to teach the names and positions of musical notes, rather than to play with sounds.

A satisfying music program is difficult to write for the preschool child. It should not require the child to mimic sounds or memorize key positions but rather should encourage exploring and playing with sound.

*Imagination: Music* offers an interesting approach to this problem. The program allows young children to compose music by moving a colored block on a musical staff. The position of the block determines pitch, and the length of the block determines the length of the note. Each time the block is moved, the corresponding note is played. This program would be within the capability of the advanced preschooler, but the emphasis on building songs with a musical staff makes it more appropriate for the older child.

The ultimate music program for preschool children should be simple to use, yet allow them to explore all sorts of sounds: rhythms, notes, whistles, vibrating tones, and various musical instruments. It should allow children to combine sounds in interesting ways. Just as children need to explore drawing before they can create representational art, children need to "scribble" with sound before they can create music. Such experimentation may be wearing on adult nerves, but it will help develop basic, premusical skills in preschool children.

## DEVELOPING YOUR OWN COMPUTER PROGRAMS

As you work with computers in the preschool, you will begin to develop definite ideas about the types of programs you would like to use with your class. This may tempt you to write your own programs. Writing effective programs for preschool children is an endeavor that requires a great degree of skill. Unless you are a skilled programmer with at least twenty-five hours per week for a year to dedicate to the endeavor, you should not expect to write commercial-quality programs. The best preschool computer programs incorporate animation and high-resolution graphics, which involve advanced programming skills. Although it is desirable to write programs to increase one's understanding of a computer, the average teacher simply does not have time to write high-quality programs.

What the skilled and concerned preschool teacher can do is contact nearby software houses that specialize in programming for children, or work with a university having a program in educational computing. Either of these sources may know of a programmer who is interested in new ideas for developing software for commercial distribution. In addition, they may be interested in finding a "beta" site for preschool software to be tested before it is finally released for commercial sale. High-quality preschool software requires a working relationship between the knowledgeable preschool educator and the skilled programmer.

The computer is a powerful and flexible educational tool for the preschool child. It requires programs that reflect the developmental concepts that undergird good preschool education. The computer can be an essential part of a preschool child's exploration of creative environments. Children love to be in control of this twentieth century tool and need good software that gives them the chance to discover new skills and adventures on their own.

## REFERENCES

Borgh, Karin, and W. Patrick Dickson. "Two Preschoolers Sharing One Microcomputer: Creating Prosocial Behavior with Hardware and Software." Edited by Patricia Campbell and Greta Fein. In *Young Children and Microcomputers*. Englewood Cliffs, N.J.: Prentice-Hall, 1986.

Clements, Douglas H. *Computers in Early and Primary Education*. Englewood Cliffs, N.J.: Prentice-Hall, 1985.

Coburn, Peter, Peter Kelman, Nancy Roberts, Thomas F. F. Snyder, Daniel H. Watt, and Cheryl Weiner. *Practical Guide to Computers in Education*. Reading, Mass.: Addison-Wesley Publishing Co., 1985.

Papert, Seymour. *Mindstorms: Children, Computers, and Powerful Ideas*. New York: Basic Books, 1980.

Staples, Betsy. "Growing Up Literate: Programs for Preschoolers, Part 5." *Creative Computing* (April 1984): 64–76.

Willis, Jerry, and Merl Miller. *Computers for Everybody*. Beaverton, Oreg.: Dilithium Press, 1984.

## CATALOGS AND INDEXES

*Beckley-Cardy Computer Education Catalog*
114 Gaither Drive
Mt. Laurel, N.J., 08054

*Follett Quality Courseware*
4506 Northwest Highway
Crystal Lake, Ill., 60014

*Only the Best: The Discriminating Software Guide for Preschool–Grade 12*
    Educational News Service
    Sacramento, Calif. 95814

*Parent-Teacher's Microcomputing Sourcebook for Children*
    R. R. Bowker Co.
    New York, N.Y. 10017

*Whole Earth Software Catalog*
    Quantum Press/Doubleday
    Garden City, N.Y. 11530

## MAGAZINES

*Antic: The Atari Resource*
    524 Second St.
    San Francisco, Calif. 94107

*Apple Education News*
    Apple Computer, Inc.
    20525 Mariani Ave.
    Cupertino, Calif. 95014

*Childhood Education*
    Association for Childhood Education International
    11141 Georgia Ave., Suite 200
    Wheaton, Md. 20902

*Commodore: The Microcomputer Magazine*
    1200 Wilson Dr.
    West Chester, Pa. 19380

*Compute!*
    324 W. Wendover Ave.
    Greensboro, N.C. 27408

*Computing Teacher*
    International Council for Computers in Education
    1787 Agate
    University of Oregon
    Eugene, Oreg. 97404

*Digest of Software Reviews: Education*
    School and Home Courseware, Inc.
    301 W. Mesa
    Fresno, Calif. 93704

*Electronic Education*
    Electronic Communication, Inc.
    Suite 220
    1311 Executive Center Drive
    Tallahasee, Fla. 32301

*Electronic Learning*
> Scholastic, Inc.
> 902 Sylvan Ave.
> Englewood Cliffs, N.J. 07632

*Enter*
> Children's Television Workshop
> One Lincoln Plaza
> New York, N.Y. 10023

*InCider*
> 80 Pine St.
> Peterborough, N.H. 03458

*InfoWorld*
> 1060 Marsh Rd., Suite C-200
> Menlo Park, Calif. 94025

*Instructor*
> 757 Third Ave.
> New York, N.Y. 10017

*PC World*
> 555 DeHaro St.
> San Francisco, Calif. 94107

*Personal Computing*
> 70 Main St.
> Peterborough, N.H. 03458

*Young Children*
> National Association for the Education of Young Children
> 1834 Connecticut Ave., N.W.
> Washington, D.C. 20009

# SOFTWARE

*Charley Brown's ABC*
> Random House
> 201 E. 50th St.
> New York, N.Y. 10022

*Delta Drawing*
> Spinnaker Software
> 215 First Street
> Cambridge, Mass. 02142

*Dinosaurs*
> Advanced Ideas, Inc.
> 2550 Ninth St., Suite 104
> Berkeley, Calif. 94710

*Early Games for Young Children: Music*
        Springboard Software, Inc.
        7807 Creekridge Circle
        Minneapolis, Minn. 55435

*Facemaker*
        Spinnaker Software Corp.
        215 First St.
        Cambridge, Mass. 02142

*Gertrude's Secrets*
        The Learning Company
        545 Middlefield Rd.
        Menlo Park, Calif. 94025

*Grandma's House*
        Spinnaker Software Corp.
        215 First Street
        Cambridge, Mass. 02142

*Imagination: Music*
        John Wiley & Sons
        605 Third Ave.
        New York, N.Y. 10158

*Jeeper's Creatures*
        Kangaroo, Inc.
        110 S. Michigan Ave., Suite 469
        Chicago, Ill. 60605

*Juggle's Rainbow*
        The Learning Company
        545 Middlefield Rd.
        Menlo Park, Calif. 94025

*Kiri's Hodge Podge*
        Dynacomp, Inc.
        1427 Monroe Ave.
        Rochester, N.Y. 14618

*Learning with Leeper*
        Sierra On-Line, Inc.
        P.O. Box 485
        Coarsegold, Calif. 93614

*Ranch*
        Spinnaker Software Corp.
        215 First St.
        Cambridge, Mass. 02142

*Sammy the Sea Serpent*
        Program Design, Inc.
        11 Idar Court
        Greenwich, Conn. 06830

*Stickybear* series

Weekly Reader Family Software
A Division of Xerox Education Publications
Middletown, Conn. 06457

# Glossary

**Accessing** The process of bringing information into the working memory of the computer from an attached device. For example, accessing the keyboard allows the computer to read the characters being typed. Accessing the disk drive turns on the disk drive and reads information (data) from the disk drive.

**Artificial intelligence** Consists of programs that make computers do things that appear to be intelligent, such as making decisions, carrying on meaningful conversations, or translating from one language to another. The earliest research on artificial intelligence was done at M.I.T.

**Assembly language (Assembler)** Programming language that requires the least amount of translation by the computer into the instruction switches built into the computer's central processing unit (chip). Many programs using complex graphics or animation are written in Assembler. Another name for assembly language is machine language programs. Writing assembly language programs requires a great deal of skill.

**Backup** A second copy of a program or disk that can be used if the original program or disk is damaged. Backups can be either a copy of the disk made by the purchaser or a second disk purchased at a reduced rate from the publisher of the software.

**BASIC** A common computer language built into most home computers. Most preschool programs are written in BASIC or a combination of BASIC and Assembler. BASIC stands for Beginners All-purpose Symbolic Instruction Code.

BASIC was originally derived from another computer language, FORTRAN. *See* Assembly language.

**Beta site** A term used for a person or place where software is tested before commercial release to the general public.

**Boot the system** Refers to loading the Disk Operating System (DOS) instructions from the disk into the memory of the computer. The Disk Operating System must be in memory before any program on the disk can be used. The term boot (or booting) comes from the saying "pulling yourself up by your bootstraps," because the Disk Operating System loads itself into the computer. The instruction built into the computer itself simply tells the computer to go to the first sector on the first track of the disk and do what ever it says. *See* DOS.

**Bug** A logical mistake in a computer program that must be found and corrected before the program will run properly. The term comes from the early days of computers when a problem in a large computer was traced to a dead moth that had short-circuited the machinery. Debugging is the process of removing bugs from a computer program. Seymour Papert's *Mindstorms: Children, Computers, and Powerful Ideas* (New York: Basic Books, 1980) has an extensive discussion of debugging as a learning strategy.

**Cap lock key** A key on a computer keyboard that changes all letters to capitals. It does not affect any other keys, such as number and punctuation keys. Some older computers, such as the APPLE II +, use a Teletype keyboard that has only capital letters and no cap lock key. This is the same keyboard found on Teletype machines in telegraph offices. *See* Shift lock key.

**Cathode-ray tube (CRT)** The picture tube in a computer monitor or TV set. Sometimes computer books will refer to the computer monitor or television connected to a computer as a CRT. *See* Monitor.

**Cartridge** A plastic box containing a single computer program. When the cartridge is plugged into a computer or video game terminal, the program can be accessed by the computer. The program itself is on a computer chip connected to the plug end of the cartridge. Cartridges are not available for all computers. *See* Accessing.

**Central Processing Unit (CPU)** The chip that contains the logical functions of the computer. It is usually the largest chip in the computer. The power of the computer depends on how many pieces (bits) of binary (base two) arithmetic the CPU can handle in calculations. The first generation of personal computers were eight-bit CPUs. Examples are the Motorola 6502 series (used in the Apple II, Commodore 64, and Atari 800 series) and the Zilog Z80 (used by most CP/M computers and the Radio Shack TRS-80s). The second generation of personal computers uses sixteen-bit processors (examples are the Intel 8086, 8088, and the 286i used in IBM PCs and IBM-compatibles and the Motorola 68000 used in the Apple Macintosh, the Commodore Amiga, and the Atari 620ST). The term CPU sometimes refers to the complete logic board(s) of the computer, including memory.

**Chip** A complex electronic circuit placed on a tiny piece of silicone. The term sometimes refers to the plastic or ceramic cases that contain a chip and provide the wires to connect the chip to larger electronic circuits.

**Command** A direction given by the computer user (or a program) to perform an action. For example, typing in DIR next to an A > prompt will list the files on the disk in drive A (on CP/M and MS DOS computers). Programs are made up of a series of commands that are performed automatically by the computer.

**Compatible** A computer that will run programs designed for another brand of computer for which a programming standard has been developed. For example, the Compaq Computer is IBM-compatible and the Franklin Computer is Apple-compatible.

**Computer** A machine that translates commands into electronic instructions that create a predictable outcome. This outcome may involve sound through a speaker, pictures on a cathode-ray tube (CRT), symbols on a printer connected to the computer, or instructions to an automobile engine. The computer is perhaps the most flexible machine ever developed, based on the breadth of its applications.

**Computer literacy** Represents a minimum level of computer knowledge and skills that a computer user should have. The computer-literate person knows the names of the parts of a computer, the function of each of the keys on the keyboard, and how to use common disk operating system commands. The goal of computer literacy is to build knowledge that will allow the computer-literate user to be comfortable with using computer software on a variety of computers.

**Copy protected disk** A computer disk which has been altered by the software manufacturer to make it difficult for a user to copy.

**Cursor** An electronic marker on the monitor that indicates where any input from the keyboard or external devices will be placed on the screen.

**Disk** A round piece of magnetically coated material that can be formatted by a disk drive to store computer programs in the form of magnetic patterns. A formatted disk consists of magnetic tracks divided into magnetic sectors. Information can be stored in each sector and retrieved by the disk operating system, which looks up the number and sector of the track. Information is stored by file name in a directory or catalog track. *See* Floppy disk; Hard disk.

**Disk drive** A device for writing on and reading disks. Disk drives consist of a motor which turns the disk, a magnetic head which moves across the disk reading the magnetically coded signals, and electronic circuits which control the mechanical parts of the disk drive and transmit the magnetic code to the computer for storage in working memory. Disk drives can either be contained in a separate box or built into the main housing of the computer.

**Disk Operating System (DOS)** The program that gives directions to the computer for accessing the disk drive. *See* Accessing; Boot the system.

**Dot matrix printer** A computer printer that forms letters or graphic images on paper by extending wires from the printer head to press against the printer ribbon. The dots in the wire correspond to the dots (pixels) creating a letter on the monitor or disk file.

**File** A program or set of information used by a program that is stored on disk or tape and can be listed by name when a directory or catalog command is given. Files may be written in high-level language, such as BASIC or LOGO, as machine language binary files, or as text files that must be read by a program.

**First-generation program** A program that does not reflect sophisticated design or programming techniques. A first-generation program is usually sequential in design (it brings up one screen at a time in a given order with a single task assigned to the screen) and assumes that the learning task is unpleasant and, therefore, should be rewarded. First-generation programs often use low-resolution graphics, which are easy to create in BASIC.

**Floppy disk** A computer storage disk consisting of a magnetically coated, round piece of mylar plastic (the same plastic used in recording tape) enclosed in a square protective envelope. Preschool programs would use either $5\frac{1}{4}$ -inch disks or the newer $3\frac{1}{5}$ -inch microdisks, which have a rigid plastic housing with a metal shutter protecting the magnetic disk from fingerprints.

**Format a disk** The process of placing magnetic tracks and sectors (or blocks) on a blank disk so that the computer can store and locate information on the disk. The program needed to format disks may be built into the disk drive (as in the case of the Commodore 64), it may be built into the Disk Operating System (Apple DOS 3.3), it may be a separate program (IBM PC DOS), or it may be included in a utility program (Apple ProDOS). No computer can read or write to an unformatted magnetic disk.

**Function keys** A special set of keys found on some computers, such as IBM compatibles and Commodore, which correspond to a program command and operate when a single function key is pressed. They are usually marked F for function and followed by a number (F8).

**Game cartridge** *See* Cartridge.

**Game cartridge port** A connection on the side or back of the computer designed to hold a game cartridge.

**Graphics** Designs created by a computer program and printed on the screen or on a printer. They may be in color.

**Hard disk** A sealed, metal disk used for program storage. The hard disk is usually installed permanently in the disk drive attached to the computer and cannot be removed. One hard disk can replace fifty to 400 floppy disks of the same size. Information can be stored more reliably on a hard disk than on floppy disks because the magnetic head that reads a hard disk does not touch the surface of the disk and the rigidity of the disk eliminates any vibrations. Hard disks are normally used for business applications that require large files. *See* Floppy disk.

**Hardware** The physical components of a computer—the electronic circuits, chips, disk drives, keyboard, printer, or the computer itself. *See* Software.

**High-resolution graphics** Pictures on the screen or printer that are created by individual, colored dots. Pictures of people or animals are usually more realistic looking in high-resolution than in low-resolution but are more difficult to program. *See* Low-resolution graphics.

**Icon** A pictoral representation often used to represent choices on a program menu. *See* menu.

**Interactive stories** Computer programs that allow the user to determine the direction of the story by making a choice presented by the program.

**Joystick** An external device for controlling cursor position on a computer screen. It consists of a rod extending from the top of a small box that is connected to the computer by a long cord. Most joysticks also have two buttons that can be pushed to initiate simple commands. Most arcade games use joysticks for program control.

**Joystick port** The place on the computer where the joystick is plugged in. It is usually found on the back or side of the computer.

**Language** A set of instructions that can be placed into the computer's memory and used by a programmer to write programs. Examples of computer languages are BASIC, Pascal, Assembler, FORTRAN, C, and COBOL. There are two types of languages: compiled and interpreted. A compiled language is translated into computer code so that it does not have to be present in memory for the computer to understand the program. Among small computers, Assembler is the most common compiled language. Interpreted languages must be present in the computer's memory because each command must be converted into the computer's machine code. BASIC is the most common interpreted language. Compiled languages execute much faster than interpreted languages and, thus, are more appropriate for games and animated graphics. *See* Assembly language; BASIC.

**Light pen** A device that looks like a ball-point pen with a cord connecting it to the computer. The light pen has a light sensitive tip that can read its position on a computer screen. Light pens are used for drawing on the screen or for making choices from a menu.

**Load the program** Refers to moving a computer program from a storage medium, such as a cartridge, tape, or disk, into the memory of the computer. When you save a program, a copy of the magnetic code is made on the disk or tape. Once a program is loaded, the disk or tape is no longer needed, unless the program is loaded in multiple stages.

**LOGO** A computer language developed at M.I.T. It is perhaps the only computer language in which commands that create graphics are easier than commands that manipulate words. Although LOGO is a very powerful computer language, it is sometimes thought of as a children's language.

**Low-resolution graphics** Graphic images made up of small squares or rectangles of color. They are sometimes referred to as block graphics. Because they require less memory than high-resolution graphics, more colors can be used. The larger size of the color blocks makes low-resolution graphics easier to program than high-resolution graphics. *See* High-resolution graphics; First-generation programs.

**Memory** The chips in the computer that hold computer programs. There are two kinds of memory: Random Access Memory (RAM), which is the working memory of the computer, and Read Only Memory (ROM). When a program is loaded into memory, it is placed in RAM. ROM contains computer programs that are a permanent part of the computer hardware. When you turn off a computer, a program in RAM will disappear, but a program in ROM will still be present in the computer. BASIC is often in ROM in personal computers.

**Menu** A set of choices presented on the screen that allows the user to choose functions in the program by pressing a key. Preschool programs may have pictorial menus, and the child chooses an option by pressing the space bar or by using the cursor when the picture appears on the screen. Other programs allow menu selection with number keys. *See* Icon.

**Monitor** A TV screen attached to a computer. Monitors are sometimes referred to as CRTs. Monitors come in a number of choices: monochromatic, composite color, and RGB. A monochromatic monitor usually consists of a monitor with white, green, or amber letters on a black background. The Macintosh computer has black letters on a white background. A composite monitor receives a TV-like signal from the computer through a thin cord. Composite monitors with sound capability can also be used as monitors for videotape machines. RGB monitors allow the computer to access directly the red, green, and blue "guns" in the picture tube for more precise control of the picture.

**Mouse** A small box connected to the computer by a long cord. Rolling the mouse on a flat surface moves the cursor position on the screen. The mouse may have one to three buttons on top for giving simple commands to the computer.

**Moving menu** A menu that automatically changes screens on the monitor. Each screen provides one choice. When the desired picture comes on the screen, it is chosen by pressing a key, such as the space bar. *See* menu.

**Off-computer activity** An activity related to the curricular goals of a computer program that does not require a computer. Examples of off-computer activities are games, toys, a typewriter, or a storybook.

**Orphan computer** A computer no longer manufactured.

**Paddle** A cursor-control device consisting of a knob on a small box with a single button. Paddles usually come in a set of two that connect to a single plug. The knob controls cursor movement. One paddle controls the horizontal movement of the cursor while the other paddle controls vertical movement. The joystick has replaced the use of paddles on most computers because it combines the function of the two paddles. *See* Joystick.

**Pascal** A computer language developed by Nicolas Wirth of Zurich, Switzerland. It is named after the French philosopher and mathematician, Blaise Pascal. A common variation of the language was developed at the University of California at San Diego and is called UCSD Pascal. *See* Language.

**Pixel** A single dot on a monitor screen. Combinations of pixels are used to form letters or high-resolution graphics. *See* High-resolution graphics.

**Power light** A light on the keyboard or front of the computer that indicates when the computer is turned on. On older Apple II computers, the power light looks like a key on the keyboard.

**Print** Has a number of meanings in the language of computers. One is to use a printer to make a paper copy (hard copy) of what would normally appear on the screen. It can also mean to show something on the screen, that is, print the data to the screen. Print is also a command in BASIC meaning print the outcome of a formula or phrase to the screen. A printout always refers to hard copy.

**Recursion** The ability of a command to repeat itself. A computer language that allows recursion may be referred to as a recursive language. LOGO and Pascal are examples of recursive languages.

**Save** Refers to storing a program or information on a disk or tape.

**Second-generation program** A program that should allow the user to move directly to various aspects of the program rather than having to move through a previously defined sequence. Second-generation programs for preschools generally use high-resolution graphics and animation in the presentation of material. Second-generation programs have many of the characteristics of first-generation programs but show greater sophistication in the design and flow of the program and in the use of graphics. *See* First-generation program; Third-generation program.

**Shift lock key** A key that changes all letter keys to uppercase and all other keys to the symbols on the top half of the key. *See* Cap lock key.

**Software** A computer program stored on a medium, such as a magnetic disk, tape, or cartridge that can be read by the computer. It is called software because, while it represents a great deal of labor, it is not tangible property but rather ideas stored in a machine-readable format. *See* Hardware.

**Sound-generation chip** A computer chip that holds and can execute the instructions in a program for creating various sounds on a speaker connected to (or part of) the computer. Some sound-generation chips are capable of creating understandable spoken words as well as four-part harmony in a music program.

**Speech-generation software** Uses the sound-generation chip to translate written words into spoken words; sometimes known as speech synthesizing. *See* Sound-generation chip.

**Storage** The medium used for saving programs for later use. *See* Disk drive.

**Stylus** A pointed stick shaped like a pencil and used for drawing on touch pads, magic slates, or cuneiform tablets. *See* Touch pad.

**System file** Commands on a disk that are used by the computer to keep track of commands available for any program used during the time the computer is turned on. An example of a system file is the Disk Operating System (DOS). System files keep track of printer commands, what kind of monitor is being used, or the type of storage medium (disk drive, tape) attached to the computer.

**Tape** Recording tape used for storing and retrieving programs. Most personal computers use a high-quality cassette tape. Tape storage is cheaper than disk, but it is harder to use and requires a significantly longer period to find and load programs.

**Third-generation program** Usually written in a compiled language and allows a great deal of flexibility. Most third-generation programs use a simple programming language to allow maximum user control.

**Touch pad** An electrically sensitive pad attached to the computer by a long wire leading to the joystick port. Pressing on the pad with a stylus or a finger will move the cursor on the screen to a corresponding position. *See* Joystick port.

**Touch screen** A transparent touch pad placed over the monitor. *See* Touch pad.

**Turnkey program** A program that starts automatically as soon as the disk is booted. The advantage of turnkey programs is that they do not require a knowledge of Disk Operating System commands to load and run the program. *See* Boot the system.

**Turtle** Either a turtle-shaped robot controlled by a LOGO program or a triangle-shaped cursor on the graphics screen of a LOGO program.

**Turtle graphics** Graphic designs created by LOGO graphic commands. While turtle graphics were originally developed as part of LOGO, they have been incorporated into programs such as *Delta Draw* and dialects of other computer languages such as UCSD Pascal. *See* Pascal.

**Word processing** Using the computer as a typewriter. The advantage of word processing is that all changes to a document are made electronically. Corrections and additions can be made without manually retyping the manuscript for each major change. Word processing also allows the user to use a spelling checker to identify misspelled words and typing mistakes. Preschool word processors are available that say the word aloud when it is entered.

**Write protect notch** A square notch on the side of $5\frac{1}{4}$ -inch floppy disks. When the notch is covered, the computer can read from the disk but it can not write to the disk. When it is uncovered, the computer can both read from the disk and write to it. The notch on the original disk should be covered when copying disks.

# Appendix A
# CHILDREN'S BOOKS

**Chapter 3, The Computer as a Playmate**
*A Funny Fish Story*, Wyle, 49
*Fish Is Fish*, Lionni, 49
*Everybody Takes a Turn*, Corey, 49
*Your Turn, Doctor*, Perez and Robison, 49

**Chapter 4, The Computer as an Alphabet Book**
*The Strawberry Look Book*, Hefter, 60
*Alphabrutes*, Nolan, 66
*Albert the Alphabetical Elephant*, Hargreaves, 66
*Dr. Seuss's ABC*, Seuss, 67
*The Bears' ABC Book*, Wild and Wild, 67
*Q Is For Duck, an Alphabet Guessing Game*, Elting and Folsom, 67

**Chapter 5, The Computer as an Abacus**
*One Bear Two Bears: the Strawberry Number Book*, Hefter, 82
*The Bears' Counting Book*, Wild and Wild, 82
*The Fancy Dress Party Counting Book*, Patience, 82
*If You Take a Pencil*, Testa, 82
*Bruno Brontosaurus*, Rubel, 85

**Chapter 6, The Computer as a Building Block**
*Inside Outside Upside Down*, Berenstain and Berenstain, 97
*Big Dog . . . Little Dog: A Bedtime Story*, Eastman, 97
*Yes and No: A Book of Opposites*, Hefter, 97
*More Opposites, Peek-a-Book*, Hill, 97
*Titch*, Hutchins, 98
*Joshua James Likes Trucks*, Petrie, 98
*Learn Opposites with the Munch Bunch*, Reed, 98
*Building a House*, Barton, 105

**Chapter 7, The Computer as a Crayon**

**Chapter 8, The Computer as a Paintbrush**

**Chapter 9, The Computer as a Chatterbox**

# Appendix B
# SOFTWARE

# Index

**199**

Janice J. Beaty, associate professor in Human Services at Elmira College, Elmira, New York, is director of the Human Services Program well as project manager of the Head Start CDA Training Program. Dr. Beaty teaches undergraduate and graduate courses in early childhood education and children's literature. She is an author of children's books (*Nufu and the Turkeyfish; Plants in His Pack; Seeker of Seaways; Guam Today and Yesterday*) as well as teacher-training textbooks (*Skills for Preschool Teachers; Observing Development of the Young Child*). Dr. Beaty has developed training materials and films for the Child Development Associate program and has traveled around the country to make presentations at CDA Training Institutes and workshops. Her interest in people of other cultures has lured her to such diverse locations as the island of Guam in the western Pacific and San Salvador Island in the Bahamas. Her present studies focus on young children's learning through self-discovery with materials in their environment.

W. Hugh Tucker is a computer applications and training consultant in Elmira, New York. His practice ranges from writing software to training employees of a major computer manufacturer. Prior to entering private practice, Dr. Tucker served on the faculties of Idaho State University and Elmira College and as visiting faculty at Syracuse University. His teaching responsibilities at all three institutions included courses on educational uses of personal computers.

Dr. Tucker has also conducted in-service courses and workshops on using personal computers in the classroom for numerous school districts, universities, community colleges, and federally funded projects.